MW01289708

HEALED!

One Couple's Journey to Healing and Beyond

Dr. Joe and Heidi Wadlinger

Tritality, Charlotte, NC, USA

Healed! One Couple's Journey to Healing and Beyond
by Dr. Joe and Heidi Wadlinger

© Copyright 2016 – Tritality. All rights reserved.

This book is protected by the copyright laws of the United States of America. This book may not be copied or reprinted for commercial gain or profit. The use of short quotations or occasional page copying for personal or group study is permitted and encouraged. Permission will be granted upon request.

Unless otherwise identified, Scripture quotations are from the "THE HOLY BIBLE, NEW KING JAMES VERSION". Copyright © 1982 by Thomas Nelson, Inc. Used by permission. All rights reserved.

Scripture quotations marked TLB are taken from The Living Bible copyright © 1971. Used by permission of Tyndale House Publishers, Inc., Carol Stream, Illinois 60188. All rights reserved.

Emphasis within Scripture quotations is authors' own. Please note that Tritality's publishing style capitalizes certain pronouns in Scripture that refer to the Father, Son and Holy Spirit, and may differ from some publishers' styles. Take notice that the name satan and his other names are not capitalized. We choose not to acknowledge him, even to the point of violating grammatical rules.

Reach us on the Internet at **www.tritality.com** or email us at **info@tritality.com**

Published by: Tritality, Charlotte, North Carolina

Cover Design by: Joseph J. Wadlinger, III

Publishing Consultant: Jeff Brewer

Title: Healed!

Subtitle: One Couple's Journey to Healing and Beyond

Authors: Joseph Allen Wadlinger & Heidi Anneliese Wadlinger

Library of Congress Catalog Number: 2016918775

ISBN: 978-1-5403824-1-2

1) Spirituality 2) Religion

For Worldwide Distribution.

First Edition Revision 1. Printed in the United States of America.

Foreword

I got an email one day asking for prayer. I knew in my heart and spirit that the woman was desperate. God said to call them (even though it was a holiday) and pray with them. When I called, I could hear screams in the background because of the intensity of the pain. I prayed and as I prayed, very little relief came.

Then what?????

And so this story unfolds...

How great are the grace and the healing power of our God! How wondrous are His ways! Few messages have the power to affect the lives of others more than a testimony of a miraculous healing experience.

Dr. Joe and Heidi Wadlinger's testimony of overcoming an incurable and life threatening disease, that filled Joe with pain for many years, can change your life too. It was an experience that tested their love for each other as well as their faith in God. It drove them to seek God in a deeper way and led finally to Joe's complete healing.

Although most of the people I pray for are healed instantly, Joe received his over a period of time. He did not give up!! He received prayer many times and sought God with tears until he was healed and whole. As his faith grew his healing progressed until all pain was gone and he could function normally. Joe and

Heidi learned a great deal during this period of their lives and in *Healed! One Couple's Journey to Healing and Beyond*, they share that knowledge they gained during this painful odyssey with you. I heartily recommend you read their story and learn all you can from their experiences.

Joan Hunter
Author/Healing Evangelist
www.joanhunter.org

Endorsements

Do you ever wonder where God is in the midst of your pain? Do you sometimes question whether God really loves you and is concerned about your situation? If some of this describes you, then you are not alone! Dr. Joe and Heidi Wadlinger describe the emotions and frustrations they experienced while waiting for the healing in Joe's body to manifest.

One of the keys they discovered is that healing is not merely an event! Often, healing can be a journey. You will love the way Joe and Heidi describe the difficult and yet glorious way the Lord led them into their journey for healing. Their book, *Healed!* is like sitting in a living room and having a conversation with them.

I recommend *Healed!* to anyone needing healing or anyone who desires to be used by God for helping others to receive healing. This book will change your life and your walk with the Lord!

Barbara Wentroble
www.barbarawentroble.com
Founder: International Breakthrough Ministries;
Breakthrough Business Network

Author: Nine books including: *Fighting for Your Prophetic Promises,*
Empowered for Your Purpose, Prophetic Intercession
and *Praying With Authority*

This book is an inspiring true story of one couple's journey from sickness to wholeness. When we first met Dr. Joe and Heidi, Joe was essentially immobile and writhing in pain from a nerve condition in his body. This condition had resulted in him giving up his career and basically being homebound. They began attending our church and immediately grabbed hold of the Word of God that promises healing to those who will believe.

It was a process, but day by day we saw improvement. I can remember the pain Joe suffered while waiting for the total manifestation of his healing, but he would not give up on the promise of God. Anytime there was an opportunity, he was there and always the first to respond to the call for prayer. Joe and Heidi spoke the promises of God, not what they saw. Even when his healing was 90% and then 95%, he would not settle for anything less than a total 100% manifested healing.

This book is a must read for anyone who is struggling with a health issue. It will build your faith as you see how God remembers His Covenant between Himself and His creation. You will see the power of confessing the Word of God over your situation to bring about God's promised end. And, you will see the Love of God in the process.

Donna Wise
Senior Pastor: Impact Church International
President: Genesis…A New Beginning
www.impactci.org

No matter where an individual is in his or her faith walk; no matter what they believe about God and His power to save, heal, and redeem; no matter how distorted a person's theology may be; a personal testimony has the ability to bring hope, even to our hardest trials and deepest pain.

Dr. Joe and Heidi Wadlinger remind us of how important and how life changing a personal testimony can be to the most hopeless situations. *Healed!* is a book filled with hope that proclaims to us all, "You too can be healed." It reminds us that Jesus really is the "Healer" and that it is the testimony of our healing that reveals the nature and character of the God we serve.

Thank you, Joe and Heidi, for never giving up, never compromising what you believe, never listening to the naysayers. Thank you for fighting the good fight and teaching us all to not give in or to settle for the plans of the enemy! Thank you for reminding us who we are in Christ! Thank you for reminding us that we too have a powerful testimony of the healing power of Jesus.

And as we tell others, we can join you in spreading hope to our generation in desperate need of the hope only found in Him!

Alex Barefoot
Lead Pastor: Eastside Community Church
www.eastsidechurch.co

Acknowledgments

I want to thank my beautiful wife, Heidi, who is a blessing from God to me. I love you with all my heart. You have always been my best friend, constant companion and confidant. Without you, not only would this book never have been written, but I would not be alive today.

To my wonderful husband, Joe, who is not only my very best friend, but a faithful prayer warrior. You so unselfishly give of yourself to me personally and to our marriage. I have even yet much to glean from your example. You hold my heart and always will.

Thanks to our sons, Joey, Jonathan and Joshua who have graciously shared us with others for all of their lives. You have grown up to be such fine godly men. And to Amanda, our amazing daughter-in-law, who is such a blessing and an answer to our prayers.

Thanks to our parents for giving us life, taking such good care of us, and encouraging us to follow our dreams. Because of you, we are.

Thanks to Joan Hunter who was instrumental in Joe's healing and encouraged us to write this book and to become ordained ministers of the Gospel of our Lord Jesus Christ. Without her love and constant friendship, our lives would not have been the same.

Thanks to our good friends, Pastors Donna and Terry Wise, for patiently walking with us through Joe's healing and mentoring us into the possibilities in God beyond where we were spiritually. We are forever grateful.

Thanks to our friend Barbara Wentroble for her incredible leadership and the prophetic words she spoke over us. They are now coming true.

Thanks to our friends Jeff and Kim Brewer who encouraged us to write this book. Without Jeff's experience in writing and publishing you would not be reading this today.

Thanks to Alex and Liz Barefoot, our pastors and our friends at Eastside Church. We are learning so much from you. Your passion for the Lord is truly refreshing.

Thanks to Randy Clark for being so compassionate and being humble enough to set us straight on healing.

This list would be endless, so to all of the people, unnamed here, who have been so instrumental in our lives; thank you for your love, prayers and encouragement. May you be truly blessed.

And most of all, *"... thanks be to God, who gives us the victory through our Lord Jesus Christ." - 1 Corinthians 15:57*

In Him, everything is Yes and Amen!

Contents

INTRODUCTION

"Lord we pray for everyone who reads this testimony. First of all we speak blessing over them in the name of Jesus. We ask that as they read these words, that You, by the power of the Holy Spirit, will guide them into all truth. That it will encourage every one of them to pursue You and Your Presence with their whole heart. And that the stories will challenge them to persevere for what Your Word says they can have through the Salvation that was purchased by Your Son. That they will know that each one is Your favorite child, and will have a renewed hope for things they have given up on. And that the lies of the enemy of our souls will be exposed, and Your Word will prevail. We speak total wholeness of body, soul and spirit to each one of them in the mighty name of Jesus. Amen and amen!"

Dr. Joe and Heidi Wadlinger

Joe

"I think you should write a book about your testimony," Jeff said. We knew he was right. My wife Heidi and I had just met Jeff and his wife Kim. We were all there finishing our final requirements for ministerial ordination in Joan Hunter Ministries based in Tomball, Texas. In the Wednesday service the night before, Joan had asked Heidi and me to share the testimony of my healing to the over 200 people that were in attendance. After that, during almost every break, people were lining up to talk to us. Many were thanking us for sharing the process we had gone through for me to be whole. It had encouraged them to persevere for healing. Others wanted to know more details. Some wanted us to pray for them, their family or their friends.

We knew our testimony had a very positive impact on those with whom we shared it, but this was the first time we had shared it with so many people at once, and the response was overwhelming. Jeff was encouraging me to write a book so that it would affect many people with whom we may never get to share our testimony face to face. But how was I supposed to do that? I only had some rudimentary knowledge about how to write and publish a book. I thought a book had to be at least two hundred pages and that seemed to me to be a daunting task. So I looked at Jeff and said, "I don't know how to do that." He reassuringly replied, "But I do." We spent much of the time we had together discussing his knowledge of the publishing business, and the fact that he had written a number of books of his own. I knew then that God had put us together for His purposes. This book is the result of those kinds of divine connections. We will tell the story from both of our vantage points. There are wonderful lessons to be learned from not only me who was physically afflicted, but also Heidi who had to take on a new role as my nurse, caregiver and spiritual intercessor.

It is difficult to just start out telling you how God healed me from such a debilitating disease without giving you some background on our lives. The faithfulness of God has been so apparent through the years, and there have been so many, what we like to call, "God sightings" along the way, that we believe this history will give you a better understanding of the nature of God and how wonderfully personal He is.

The Greek word *sozo* is sometimes translated in the New Testament as healed. An example is the woman with the issue of blood that was healed by Jesus.

"But Jesus turned around, and when He saw her He said, "Be of good cheer, daughter; your faith has made you well (sozo)." And the woman was made well (sozo) from that hour." - Matthew 9:22

Sozo means more than just to make well physically. Strong's says that sozo means "heal, preserve, save (self), do well, be (make) whole."

Here is an example of the word sozo being translated as saved.

"For God sent not his Son into the world to condemn the world; but that the world through him might be saved (sozo)." - John 3:17

So as we can see when Jesus saved the world, he literally was making the world "whole" again. He came to make His children whole spiritually, mentally, emotionally and physically, which includes our bodies as well as our finances. (See 2 Corinthians 8:9)

With that understanding we will start off with a short autobiography of our lives hitting all the highlights that show how God is a personal God and interested in every aspect of our lives.

1

BACKGROUND

Joe

I was born Joseph Allen Wadlinger in New Castle, Pennsylvania to my wonderful parents Joseph and Frances on Saint Patrick's Day in a snowstorm. My father barely got to the hospital in time. After he got over the shock of my cone shaped head, as a result of my time in the birth canal, he welcomed me into the family as their first child. My parents could not be any more different. My father, the 11th of 12 children and the last boy of 6, comes from a very German Catholic background. One of his sisters had even dedicated her life as a nun. My mother, on the other hand, comes from a Pentecostal Italian family where she was one of 6 and the middle girl of 3.

My sister Deborah was born 2½ years later and our family was complete. My parents provided a warm, loving and encouraging environment for us to grow up in. We moved to Kettering, Ohio when I was 6 years old and I spent my elementary school years there in a neighborhood full of children around my own age. Even though my family went to a Pentecostal church, I got saved that same year at vacation bible school in a friend's

Methodist church. I remember very distinctly, running up to my mother and saying, "Mommy, I just asked Jesus into my heart." I did all the typical things young boys do and because my father was an engineer, I developed a love for all kinds of mechanical, audio and video things.

We moved to Troy, Michigan when I was in 7th grade and I finished up my junior and senior high school years there. I was very involved in photography, drama, choir and the Honor Society as well as being the head of the Audiovisual Department in my senior year. I was honored to be salutatorian of my high school class. I attended Wayne State University in Detroit where I graduated Phi Beta Kappa and Phi Lambda Upsilon with a degree in chemistry and went on to the Medical School to earn my medical degree.

I met my wife Heidi in junior high school and she became one of my best friends. Early on we mostly dated other people because we really had little romantic interest in each other. We did date each other a few times and even went to the senior prom and many other important events together, but it never developed into anything lasting.

One day, in the summer between my first and second year of medical school, I was praying and asking the Lord about who I would marry one day. I had been praying for many years for that special woman that God would reveal to me at a future date. I would pray that He would save her, fill her with His Holy Spirit, prepare her to be my wife and also prepare me to be her husband.

This time, unexpectedly, He gave an answer. He said, "You are to marry Heidi." His voice was as clear as if He was standing right there in the room talking to me. I didn't hear it audibly, but in my spirit it was clearer than even that. Immediately a love like I had never had for anyone else before sprang up inside of my heart and I knew that she was the one. As soon as I got back into town I went straight to her house and asked her if we could start going out together. She said she was currently dating someone else. I was so sure of what God had spoken to me that I said, "Well when you are through with him, I'll be here." Within a very short time we were dating, got engaged and then married. On our wedding day we had known each other for over nine years.

After we had been married for a few years I received my medical degree and we moved to Charlotte, North Carolina where I started my internship. About half way through I realized that patient care was not where I was supposed to be and instead got a job in a large healthcare computer company that developed software for doctor's offices and hospitals. I knew in my heart that this was where God wanted me to be. I could use my medical knowledge and also my technical talents in this arena.

Meanwhile, Heidi and I wanted to have children. We had been trying for a long time and the wait was agonizing, especially for her. It seemed like everyone around us was getting pregnant but us. Maybe it was because I had always prayed that the Lord would only give us children who would serve Him. I asked that we would never lose even one of our descendants to the enemy. We continued praying and trusting God because we knew that children are a gift from the Lord and our inheritance. Once, during that time, we were offered a baby to adopt and were seriously considering it. We took it to the Lord and He said, "No, this one is not yours." We knew at that point God had other plans in store.

One day while I was driving to the airport to fly out to California for a business trip, I stopped at a red light. Suddenly I had an open vision. In my arms was a little baby boy with blue eyes. This was a little strange because both Heidi and I have hazel-brown eyes, so blue eyes would not be what I would have expected. I heard the Lord in my spirit say that he would be like a Jeremiah and to name him such. Immediately I called Heidi at home and told her she was pregnant with a little boy with blue eyes. She said, "I am not! I know my own body and I would know if I was pregnant!" I knew by the hurt tone of her voice that she felt this was a cruel thing to say, raising her expectations without physical proof after all we had been through waiting on a child. But just like when God spoke to me about marrying her, I knew this was Him.

Later, after I had gotten to my hotel, I received a call. It was Heidi. "I just wanted to let you know that you were right," she said apologetically but with excitement, "I did a home pregnancy test and I am pregnant!" That boy, with blue eyes, was our first son and we named him Joseph Jeremy. (In the KJV of the New Testament in Matthew 27:9 it refers to Jeremiah as the prophet Jeremy.) Jeremiah was called the weeping prophet and Joey, as he likes to be called, has the most compassion for people of anyone in our family. Before our other two sons were born, the Lord would tell me that Heidi was pregnant before she knew, but it didn't come in a vision like that one. Our other two sons, who have <u>brown</u> eyes, are Jonathan David and Joshua Paul. All three are wonderful men who love the Lord. It is always better to wait on the Lord. Most often His perfect timing is not ours.

After a number of years working for the healthcare computing company and another small computing company, two of my friends and I started our own business building data collection software for various industries. The Lord really blessed us, and at one time our company employed 21 people and did several million dollars in sales in our peak year. Due to the wisdom of the Holy Spirit we were able to do for our customers what other companies had failed at. Whenever we needed revenue I would go to the Lord in prayer and He would answer. It used to be a joke between my business partner and me. He would say, "Joe, you can stop praying now, we have more work than we can handle."

Heidi

I grew up as Heidi Anneliese Boden, the daughter of two German immigrant parents. My father Heinz came from a family of 2 boys and 1 girl. He contracted polio when he was a child and has had to deal with that physical challenge all his life. He taught me how to persevere and to never give up even in the hard times. He is a very strong man with strong convictions. When he married my mother, he adopted me and gave me his name. It was not until I was 23 years old that I knew about this because he has always treated me like his very own daughter. My mother Waltraud had one sister who was my godmother, and a half-brother and a half-sister from my grandfather's first marriage. Wally, as my mother was called, grew up to become independent and self reliant and was a very talented seamstress. My brother Hans was born one year after me and we lived in Michigan most of our lives.

I grew up loving music. My parents always had German music playing in our home. I learned to play the guitar when I was twelve and went on to learn piano and bass guitar. I sang everywhere: school, church, honors choir, ensembles, madrigals and singing groups. My family was actively involved in Community Theater. My mother was very talented and made beautiful costumes. My father was gifted at electronics, stage lighting and sound. My brother and I loved singing and acting. In high school I was involved in choir and many dramas. I even co-starred in my junior year in the musical "Oklahoma" and was the star of the musical in my senior year.

I met Joe in junior high, but we became close and lasting friends in 8th grade because of algebra class. I was struggling to understand the math, unlike Joe who would correct the teacher's math problems written on the chalkboard. I asked if he would help me and after that we would spend hours on the phone almost every night doing our algebra problems together. I said almost every night because on Wednesdays he went to church. That was very strange to me. I thought you only had to go to church on Sunday.

In our senior year Joe's sister Debbie asked me if I wanted to join their Christian singing group. The only Christian music I knew about sounded like funeral music. Fortunately, the music they were singing was contemporary Christian music. "Wow," I thought, "This is good, I'm in." They invited me to their church, which was a Pentecostal denomination, and as the service progressed I wondered what I had gotten myself into. People were raising their hands and singing, giving prophecies and speaking in other languages in prayer. Joe and Debbie say that I actually looked very concerned and slid down in my seat. I couldn't wait to get out of there. But one thing kept me coming back. These people really seemed to believe in Jesus. For the first time in my life I asked Jesus to come into my life, was baptized in water and filled with the Holy Spirit. Jesus has been my Lord ever since.

I was nineteen years old and struggling with God's will for my life I when asked the Lord, "Am I supposed to stay single all my life or get married?" He said to me, "You are going to marry Joe Wadlinger." An immediate peace came over me and

I put it out of my mind. We weren't even dating then. I didn't remember that the Lord had said that to me until He reminded me after Joe asked me to marry him.

At the time Joe and I started dating, the relationship I had with my parents was very strained. When I became a Christian, I think my mom and dad thought I had joined a cult. Since their form of Christianity and mine were very different, there was an attitude I had developed in that area that bordered on rebellion. This caused our communication to be contentious. Joe picked up on this and told me that if we were to continue our relationship, then I needed to humble myself and ask my parents to forgive me for that attitude.

One day when I was sitting at the kitchen table with my mom and dad, I told them how wrong I had been and asked for their forgiveness. Immediately it felt as if a giant wall between us had crumbled and mutual respect rose in its place. Communication became easier and our relationship grew in trust.

While Joe and I were still dating, my parents surprised me and said they had decided to move from Michigan and settle in the Carolinas. My father felt it would be better for his health. I was torn as to what I should do. Should I stay there in Michigan or go with them? I humbled myself, prayed for God to give my parents wisdom, and asked my mom and dad what they wanted me to do. "We think you have a future here with Joe," they said, "You should stay here."

Joe and I got married in his second year of medical school. I had been working as a dental technician and supported us through Joe's last years of school. When he decided to not become a practicing physician I was relieved. I really was not excited about being married to a doctor. At that time I had heard that many doctor's families suffered from the long hours and stress.

I continued working even after our first son Joey was born because we needed the extra income. I never said anything to Joe, but I was becoming increasingly grieved that I had to leave Joey at the babysitter's house 5 days a week. I started asking the Lord that when Joey reached the age of 2, that He would let me quit my job and be a stay-at-home Mom.

One day, just before Joey was 2 years old, Joe said, "I have been thinking. I believe that I'm now making enough at my job, that when Joey turns 2 you can quit your job and stay home with him." Tears started to well up in my eyes. The Lord had heard my prayers and had answered them exactly how I had asked Him. Joe had no clue as to my desire or the time frame I had asked God for. We were amazed at the goodness of God and how He had orchestrated everything to make this happen.

God has always provided for us both naturally and supernaturally. One story I like tell is a period in our lives where we were getting checks and money almost every week from all sorts of unexpected places. Joe would walk in and say, "Here's another one," and we would laugh in amazement. When the checks stopped we had tens of thousands of dollars in our savings account. We were dreaming up things that we could do with the money. We could put on a new room on the house, go on a trip, or give it away. We prayed and God said, "No, put it away and keep it for a year and if you still have it, you are free to do what you want with it." Little did we know, but He did, that Joe would not be taking a salary from his company for almost 2½ years. We lived off of that blessing for all of that time. When his salary started again we had about $200 left in that account. The verse in Matthew 6:8b where Jesus says, *"For your Father knows the things you have need of before you ask Him,"* became very real to us and is still a word we live by today.

Joe has always been a strong spiritual leader in our home. That allowed me to relax under that spiritual umbrella and not do a lot of prayer and Bible study on my own. Even though my faith was strong, I was not prepared for what was to come next.

2

THE PAIN BEGINS

Joe

I had always been a very healthy adult. But that began to change in 2004. I was spending long hours at work building our company and programming many hours straight in a day and began having lower back problems. That year, the sciatic pain had become so severe in my right leg that I could only work half days and had to come home and lie down as the pain throbbed. I went to see a neurosurgeon who diagnosed that I had a bulging disk. He asked me what kind of chair I sat in to program at work and what my posture was like. I told him that I sat in a high back executive chair and kind of slid down and slouched forming a "C" with my back. He showed me the MRI. Because of my posture I had deformed my back and made it susceptible to this kind of injury. He gave me two options, physical therapy or surgery. Since my father had surgery when he was about my age for a similar thing, and it fixed the problem, I opted for the surgery.

After the surgery the pain diminished significantly and I went home to recover, but I made a major mistake that being a doctor I should have known not to. I felt guilty just staying home and allowing myself to recover so I got a laptop, laid in our big leather recliner on a heating pad and starting programming again for work. The heating pad felt good, but by just laying there my back muscles deteriorated instead of strengthened and my spine didn't have the benefit of exercise to strengthen the bones and surrounding muscles and ligaments to keep the same thing from happening again. I had just compounded the problem.

Less than a year later, after working out on a stair stepper, I felt a searing pain worse than I ever had before going from my lower back to my big toe on my right foot. I had to lay perfectly straight on my back. If I bent at all the pain felt like someone had clamped the two leads of an arc welder from my back to my foot. The pain was so bad that my father, my wife and my sons had to make me a makeshift stretcher and carry me into the neurosurgeon's office. He took one look and sent me straight over to the hospital for emergency surgery. Just before the surgery I had an MRI. The technician said that the disc had "blown out" and a large piece had lodged in my spinal canal and was pressing on my spinal column causing the pain. The surgery was successful and the searing pain went away. The neurosurgeon said the disk fragments were among the largest he had ever seen. One was about the size of a quarter. But I still had not learned my lesson and continued programming from the recliner with a heating pad on my lower spine.

I never returned to normal and there was still weakness and mild pain in my back, leg and gluteal muscles. Somehow, around this time, I had come down with walking pneumonia that was undiagnosed for almost a year. When it was finally found and treated, it had so drained my body, that I became severely depressed. Not remembering that it takes several months to get over the effects of pneumonia, I asked my personal physician to put me on antidepressants. I reacted terribly with incredible anxiety and strange sensations in my body, but I was afraid to get off of the medication completely even though the amount I was taking was minimal.

I went back to my neurosurgeon complaining about the residual pain. He said that he would not do another surgery but would send me to a hospital based pain clinic for evaluation. The physician at the pain clinic happened to be the head doctor there. He recommended that they inject my spine with a corticosteroid medication that might help alleviate my pain. The procedure technically went well and he was pleased. I went home to bed with an ice pack on my back as the doctor had prescribed. Suddenly, it felt like someone took a hot poker and thrust it into my lower back. It was pain like I had never experienced before in my entire life. I knew there was a problem and I began weeping and cried out, "What have I done?"

The pain began extending from my lower spine and grew to encompass my entire right leg. It was like having someone pour hot lava, not only on my skin, but deep inside my back and in the muscles, nerves and bones of my leg. There was no comfortable position that I could put myself in. Sitting was the worst. I had to stand to eat, but I had to do that quickly and lie down or the pain would overwhelm me. The position where I had the least pain was lying on my stomach, so we purchased a massage table so I could do that more comfortably.

We called the doctor and went back to the pain clinic as soon as we could. When the doctor saw me he said, with tears welling up in his eyes, "Oh my, I am so sorry, I did this to you!" Little did we know that 1 in about 3000 patients can have this kind of reaction to corticosteroid injections in the spine.

This is what the site DrugLib.com says about this particular medication: *(Underlines are added for emphasis)*.

Warning: This product contains benzyl alcohol, which is potentially <u>toxic</u> when administered locally to <u>neural tissue</u>. *(Neural tissue is the brain, spinal cord and nerves)*

Adverse Reactions: Intrathecal/Epidural: <u>Arachnoiditis</u>, bowel/bladder dysfunction, headache, meningitis, parapareisis / paraplegia, seizures, <u>sensory disturbances</u>. *(Epidural is basically the space around the spinal cord).*

Even though physicians use this medication to inject into the spine to reduce inflammation, it is an "off-label" usage. This means that physicians have found it effective even though the FDA has not specifically approved it for that use. Thousands upon thousands of people have had this procedure done with no adverse effects. I happened to be one of the unfortunate few.

Heidi

I could see that the doctor, also a Christian, was so remorseful and was probably wondering if we were going to bring some kind of a lawsuit. I turned to him and said, "Doctor, we know this was not your fault and we don't hold you responsible. We just want you to know that." The expression of relief on his face was tangible and from that moment on he always made himself available to us.

Joe

I was still hoping that the doctors would find an answer. We went back to the pain clinic often and I begged the doctors to help me. I had multiple MRIs to see what might be wrong. Even though my neurosurgeon was unwilling to do another back surgery, I was desperate. I knew that I had some relief before and maybe, just maybe, I would get it again. Another neurosurgeon had mercy on me and scheduled a third back surgery to remove any scar tissue that may be impinging on my nerves and causing the pain. After the surgery the doctor told Heidi, "The surgery went well. There was a lot of scar tissue in there. We got it all out. I believe he is going to feel much better." But the surgery didn't seem to help at all and the pain only got worse. We were running out of options.

Among the many MRIs I had at this time, there was one that identified the real problem. The radiologist reported that it looked like I might have an incurable condition called arachnoiditis. This finding was dismissed by my pain specialist. When I brought it to his attention, he said that he didn't believe that diagnosis was correct. But as I detailed above, this is one of the rare adverse reactions to injecting corticosteroids into the spine.

From the NIH.gov website:
http://www.ninds.nih.gov/disorders/arachnoiditis/arachnoidit is.htm.
(Underlines are added for emphasis)

What is Arachnoiditis?

Arachnoiditis describes a pain disorder caused by the inflammation of the arachnoid, one of the membranes that surround and protect the nerves of the spinal cord. The arachnoid can become inflamed because of an irritation from chemicals, infection from bacteria or viruses, as the result of direct injury to the spine, chronic compression of spinal nerves, or complications from spinal surgery or other invasive spinal procedures. Inflammation can sometimes lead to the formation of scar tissue and adhesions, which cause the spinal nerves to "stick" together. If arachnoiditis begins to interfere with the function of one or more of these nerves, it can cause a number of symptoms, including numbness, tingling, and a characteristic stinging and burning pain in the lower back or legs. Some people with arachnoiditis will have debilitating muscle cramps, twitches, or spasms. It may also affect bladder, bowel, and sexual function. In severe cases, arachnoiditis may cause paralysis of the lower limbs.

Is there any treatment?

Arachnoiditis remains a difficult condition to treat, and long-term outcomes are unpredictable. Most treatments for arachnoiditis are focused on pain relief and the improvement of symptoms that impair daily function. A regimen of pain management, physiotherapy, exercise, and psychotherapy is often recommended. Surgical intervention is controversial since the outcomes are generally poor and provide only short-term relief.

What is the prognosis?

Arachnoiditis is a disorder that causes chronic pain and neurological deficits and does not improve significantly with treatment. Surgery may only provide temporary relief. The outlook for someone with Arachnoiditis is complicated by the fact that the disorder has no predictable pattern or severity of symptoms.

Heidi

The doctors had tried everything to correct what they thought was the problem. They were already trying medications to reduce or mask the pain. It seemed like every medication they tried either didn't work at all or caused side effects Joe could not tolerate. The next treatment suggestion was to put a programmable nerve stimulator in Joe's spine to try to cover the pain up with a different sensation.

A new doctor had come to run the pain clinic. He was world renowned in the placement and management of nerve stimulators. He was sure this would be the answer to our dilemma. This stimulator had worked for thousands of others with intractable nerve pain. I told Joe that I was not in favor of this operation. Something inside of me felt like it would not work for him, but he was determined that this was the only thing he had not tried and because of his desperation I agreed to let the doctor put it in.

During the first surgery Joe was blissfully in sedated sleep. Only one wire was placed and Joe felt it didn't give him any relief. The doctor decided to do another operation to put in a second wire. This time he did it with Joe awake and with minimal anesthesia so he could try to place the lead where Joe said the pain was most severe. Joe said that he could feel the wire being pushed up his spinal cord to its final position. The feeling was extremely uncomfortable and even eerie.

But even after those two surgeries to place the stimulator wires in his spine, Joe was not to be one of the successes. Instead of reducing the pain, it just added a feeling on top of the pain that felt like a mild vibrating electrical shock. Joe was extremely disillusioned and became even more depressed. We finally asked the surgeon to remove the stimulator and the wires, which took a third surgery, because they were not doing any good.

After this surgery the doctor came into the recovery room and took me aside. "I think you need to take him to a psychiatrist," he said. I was indignant. "You don't even know this man," I said, "This is not at all who he is. This is all a reaction to the pain and medications." We never went back to the pain clinic to see this doctor again.

3

IT GETS WORSE

Joe

The next two years were a living hell for me and a nightmare for Heidi and my family. The pain only got worse and because I was in bed most of the day I was losing muscle size and strength. My ligaments grew weaker and my spine was not being supported properly. This just aggravated the burning pain and my joints would go out of place and become inflamed adding more pain in other parts of my body. The original pain doctor tried me on NSAIDs, oral corticosteroids, narcotics, antidepressants, muscles relaxers and many other types of medications. He even tried some medications that they give to cancer patients to ease their discomfort but nothing touched the intractable pain. Many of the medications caused nausea, heart palpitations, anxiety, nightmares, depression, and other psychological and physical symptoms. I was continually depressed and my physician was trying everything he knew to do, but to no avail.

My body was constantly focused on the excruciating pain since it never let up. Just imagine that you just smashed your thumb with a hammer. In that instant you would drop the hammer, grit your teeth and grab your thumb tightly in the other hand. All you would care about is the thumb and the pain. Every thought in your brain would be directed toward that pain. If someone were to ask you even a simple question in that moment, like what 2+2 is, you probably wouldn't be able to answer or even care. It's all about the pain. Normally that intenseness only lasts for a little while, and then reduces into a dull ache and eventually goes away in a few days. Now imagine if nerve pain more intense than that encompassed your entire lower body and never went away. If you can image that, then you will understand in a small measure what I was going through.

Any situation that took even a small amount of brainpower would literally cause the pain to increase in intensity as my mind would have to give up focusing on mentally managing the pain to focus on something else. My stress hormones were depleted and my brain felt the brunt of trying to manage everything by itself. I remember one situation that is a good example of what would happen on a regular basis. It was tax time. I had been doing my own taxes since I was a teenager and even though it was intense and stressful each year, it was just a marathon session and got done.

This year it was different. I had to direct my wife and my mother to collect all the paperwork, organize it, and then enter it into the tax program that I normally used. I would get up out of bed, go into the room where they were working, lie down again, and then guide them through the process for about an hour maybe two. Then my brain would exhaust, my stress and pain would go through the roof, I would excuse myself with tears in my eyes and tell them I needed to go lay down again to allow my brain to return to managing the pain for a while, and then I could come back. That process happened over and over again until it was finally done. It seemed to me to take forever and after that I had to allow my body to recover for a long while. Any decision-making was like this and the big decisions took even a larger toll.

Because of my condition I could no longer work, even at home. Fortunately my business had purchased long-term disability insurance, which I qualified for, and after that ran out, Social Security quickly put me on disability. Usually it takes a long time to get approved for disability, but because arachnoiditis is so severe and because the doctor wrote a report to them that said that I would never be able to work again, there was no resistance at all. Unfortunately the amount of money I received from disability was not enough to support our high medical expenditures, medical insurance and the expenses for a family of five. My parents graciously and lovingly picked up the slack and supported us both financially and physically. The Lord even impressed on an anonymous couple in our church to give us $1000! The Lord Who Provides, Jehovah Jireh, never failed us and we were never in lack. Praise His Name.

The people of my church rallied around us in prayer especially in the first months. But as time went on I think they ran out of answers as to how to pray for me. A few were faithful to visit whenever they could with encouragement. Some said that I was like Job and God had put me through this so that He could show His sovereignty. Some said that we didn't have enough faith. A few suggested that I just "pull myself up by my bootstraps" and just go about my day as though I was already healed and just ignore the pain. But most didn't know what to do and eventually I felt lonely and abandoned. Part of that was my own fault because most of the time I didn't even feel well enough to have anyone visit and encouraged Heidi to tell them not to come, even if they were going to pray for me.

I began to feel abandoned by God too. Didn't He see me? Didn't He know I was in so much pain? Why was I singled out for this? I was a better Christian than most people I knew. Hey I had even been a deacon and an elder. I had taught Sunday school for years. I had been faithful to always pay my tithes and give offerings. I went to church almost every time the doors were open and probably was at more services than the pastor. Didn't God know that? I even started saving up pills to commit suicide and I didn't even care what God thought about it. I mean, God had abandoned me anyway. Why did I think I would even make it into Heaven? I must not be even good enough to be healed. Obviously I was in a deep depression and my ability to trust God had gone the way of my pain.

It had gotten so bad that I would not let Heidi leave the house. The pain would spike many times during the day especially when the weather changed and the barometer would either rise or fall. She could tell you when it was about to rain because the pain would get so bad that I would put a pillow over my face and scream. I was so afraid, that I would not let her go out of the house unless it was on my terms. I would say, "I'm going to lie in bed until 11 am and pretend you are here. Then I will call out to you and I will expect you to come. If you leave, please don't let me know. Just make sure you are back by eleven or I don't know what I will do."

Heidi

When I was home, I would help Joe out to the massage table where I would spend hours massaging his muscles to release the spasms and reduce the pain. Once a week Joe's mother would come over and stay with him while I ran errands. There were several times she had to call me to come home because she could not stand watching him suffer. I had to do all of this and take care of 3 sons, one dog and an entire household as well. I felt trapped, but I never let on. When Joe would lose hope I would say, "If I have to throw you over my shoulder and carry you across the finish line we are going to see you healed."

I continued to encourage myself in the Lord. I cannot count the number of times he would look pitifully into my eyes and say, "You won't leave me will you?" My answer was always firm and resolute. "When we married," I would proclaim, "I took wedding vows that said for richer or poorer and in sickness and in health. I meant them then and I still mean them now, so I'm not going anywhere. You are stuck with me." I was resolute, even though there were many times I felt like just getting in a car and driving away for good.

What was even more significant to me was not having Joe's spiritual leadership anymore. He was unsure and wavering. The medications were taking their toll on his brain. Most times he couldn't even put together a complete sentence. He was forgetful and repeated himself all the time. And, he questioned what he had believed about God all of his life. It was now up to me to take the lead and spend time with God for all of us. My family was suffering and if I didn't get direction from the Lord it was going to be in shambles. I spent more time in the Word and in prayer than I ever had in my entire life. I would get up early and stay up late trying to find the answers we needed.

There were times Joe and I would pray 8, 10, or even 12 hours a day. We would speak in tongues for hours. We played worship music all day long and worshiped as much as we were able. We read the Bible all the time. We had scripture verses taped everywhere and prayer cloths pinned to his clothes and pillowcase. Joe would tell me that it seemed like God didn't care or wasn't even there. He started to think that he had believed a lie about God and had been brainwashed by the church. He was asking, "Was God real, or if He was, did He not even care about us?"

I started to wonder if we were missing something. My faith was still strong. "I think we should throw out everything we know about healing and start from scratch," I said to Joe, "Let's start with what the Bible says and then start reading books from people who experienced the healing power of God in their lives and ministries." His mother purchased us a subscription to a satellite network that featured Christian TV channels and we started watching every healing evangelist program we could find. I believe the Spirit of God guided us as to which programs to watch that would encourage us that healing was real.

The biggest breakthroughs were from the books we found on healing that had been written decades before. These men and women were the pioneers in bringing back healing to the church. Before their time (and even today) there were those who said that the kind of healing we see in the Bible died out with the Apostles. They said that God is sovereign and He heals who He wants, when He wants, but our direct prayers have little to do with whether someone is healed or not. These pioneers challenged that theology and saw incredible miracles by using the authority that Christ Jesus has given to us.

"And the glory which You gave Me I have given them, that they may be one just as We are one: I in them, and You in Me; that they may be made perfect in one, and that the world may know that You have sent Me, and have loved them as You have loved Me." - John 17:22-23

These pioneers laid hands on the sick and saw them miraculously recover. Many of them came out of the early Pentecostal movement that started with the Azusa Street revival. The walls of their meetings were lined with wheelchairs and crutches, casts and braces. Jesus' command for us to "Heal the sick, raise the dead, cast out devils and cleanse lepers" was taken seriously and showed the Kingdom of Heaven really was at hand. Everyone who came to Jesus was healed and He gave us that authority and they believed it and demonstrated it.

One of the books that we read and led us to many others was *God's General's* by Roberts Liardon. In its pages we read about those people and "why they succeeded and why some failed." We read about John Alexander Dowie, Maria Woodworth-Etter, Evan Roberts, Charles Parham, William J. Seymour (of the Asuza Street revival), John G. Lake (our personal favorite), Aimee Semple McPherson, Smith Wigglesworth, Kathryn Kuhlman, and many more. Granted, none of these people were perfect, and they had their struggles, and some ended very poorly, but they were seeing people, like Joe and worse, healed!

We began devouring these resources. I read to Joe from these books and also the verses from the Bible that spoke about healing. I walked him out to the massage table and worked on him while we watched people on television teaching on healing and the testimonies of people who were being healed. We had entered a whole new realm. We had never heard of most of these people before and we marveled that after all our years in Christianity this had been hidden from us. A treasure that had been buried was now found and we were digging it up.

Like I said previously, one of the ministers who was our personal favorite to read about was John G. Lake. He died in 1935, but his legacy lives on in a ministry called "Healing Rooms." While he was alive his healing rooms <u>documented</u> over 100,000 healings. He was a dynamic man and gave up a lucrative career to pursue God and minister His healing power all over the world. Then there was Smith Wigglesworth, a plumber by trade, who not only saw incredible healings, but raised people from the dead by the power of God. This only egged us on that healing was possible for Joe and we started to look for modern day people through whom true miracles were happening.

Reading about John G. Lake started me thinking a lot about the Healing Rooms. While lying in bed one night I had an urge to look it up on the Internet. Low and behold they were still in existence today and there were some in our area. We started going to one in Charlotte and the people there were so encouraging and prayed for Joe with such compassion. Because Joe could not sit without pain, I would load him into the back seat of the car where he could lie down until we got there. Then I would carry in an exercise mat and he would lay on it while we prayed and believed God. I can't say that anything physical happened at that time, but our faith got considerably stronger and Joe was much encouraged because of that.

Since it was such an incredible struggle for Joe to go to the Healing Rooms, he would not let me take him there as much as I would have liked. They had a healing school and I decided I needed to go. Joe agreed. These people knew things that I needed to know. In my conversations with the people at the Healing Rooms in Charlotte, I heard about a ministry in Redding California. Bethel Church was that place and the national head of the Healing Rooms Ministries, Cal Pierce, had been an elder and a board member there. The senior pastor,

Bill Johnson, really believes in healing and is a dynamic teacher of God's Word. I looked him up on the Internet and we started watching him preach and tell numerous stories of people being healed, not only through him, but through the leaders and even the members of his church. The testimonies were amazing as people with almost every type of disease imaginable were being healed and restored. I remember Joe saying to me, "Do you think that those healings are real?" Joe needed something to hang onto and he needed it to be real. We called the church and the youth pastor prayed for us and said they would add Joe to their prayer list. We considered going there, but the trip would have been too much for Joe to handle.

I realized through these encounters that the healing power of God had not gone out with the Apostles. It was real and it was happening in many places on a regular basis by the power of prayer. And there was a difference in the prayers. When these people prayed, they did it with authority. They didn't ask God to heal the person; they spoke to the disease or infirmity with authority and commanded what they wanted. This was new to us. Instead of saying something like, "Father, I ask you to heal Joe's back in the name of Jesus," they would say, "In the name of Jesus, I speak to this back to be healed. Pain and inflammation go! Nerves, vertebrate, muscles and discs be made whole. Body, line up with the Word of God!" Wow, I could never remember anyone praying like that. They prayed as though THEY had the authority to heal in the name of Jesus. And it was working.

Joe

We started looking in the Word of God. How did Jesus heal? How did the disciples heal? And you know what we found? They did it the same way. As we studied we could not find one place in the New Testament where Jesus, the Apostles or anyone else ever asked the Father to do the healing. They healed using the authority given by the Father to Jesus, who in turn gave that authority to them.

Here are some examples from Jesus:

The Madman at Capernaum - Mark 1:23-27

"Now there was a man in their synagogue with an unclean spirit. And he cried out, saying, 'Let us alone! What have we to do with You, Jesus of Nazareth? Did You come to destroy us? I know who You are - the Holy One of God!"

But Jesus rebuked him, saying, 'Be quiet, and come out of him!' And when the unclean spirit had convulsed him and cried out with a loud voice, he came out of him. Then they were all amazed, so that they questioned among themselves, saying, 'What is this? What new doctrine is this? For with authority He commands even the unclean spirits, and they obey Him.'"

Peter's mother-in law - Matthew 8:14-17

"And when Jesus was come into Peter's house, he saw his wife's mother laid, and sick of a fever. And he touched her hand, and the fever left her: and she arose, and ministered unto them.

When the even was come, they brought unto him many that were possessed with devils: and he cast out the spirits with his word, and healed all that were sick: that it might be fulfilled which was spoken by Esaias the prophet, saying, Himself took our infirmities, and bare our sicknesses."

The Leper - Matthew 8:1-4
"When He had come down from the mountain, great multitudes followed Him. And behold, a leper came and worshiped Him, saying, 'Lord, if You are willing, You can make me clean.' Then Jesus put out His hand and touched him, saying, 'I am willing; be cleansed.' Immediately his leprosy was cleansed."

Here are some examples from the Disciples:

Success of the Seventy - Luke 10:8, 9 & 17
"Whatever city you enter, and they receive you, eat such things as are set before you. And heal the sick there, and say to them, 'The kingdom of God has come near to you.'

And the seventy returned again with joy, saying, Lord, even the demons are subject unto us* through thy name."

* Notice they said "us".

Man at the Gate Beautiful - Acts 3:6-8
"Then Peter said, 'Silver or gold I do not have, but what I* have I* give you. In the name of Jesus Christ of Nazareth, walk.' Taking him by the right hand, he helped him up, and instantly the man's feet and ankles became strong. He jumped to his feet and began to walk"

* Notice he said "I" twice.

Aeneas Healed - Acts 9:33-35

"There he found a certain man named Aeneas, who had been bedridden eight years and was paralyzed. And Peter said to him, 'Aeneas, Jesus the Christ heals you. Arise and make your bed.' Then he arose immediately. So all who dwelt at Lydda and Sharon saw him and turned to the Lord."

Tabitha Raised From the Dead - Acts 9:36-41

"And it came to pass in those days, that she was sick, and died: whom when they had washed, they laid her in an upper chamber...But Peter put them all forth, and kneeled down, and prayed; and turning him to the body said, Tabitha, arise. And she opened her eyes: and when she saw Peter, she sat up. And he gave her his hand, and lifted her up, and when he had called the saints and widows, presented her alive."

Notice that Peter prayed first. I believe that Peter knew that she was with the Lord and was asking God if He really wanted her to come back to the earth before he took authority over death. Take notice that it was after Peter prayed that he turned toward the body and spoke the command for her to arise. There are numerous examples of praying with authority like this in the New Testament, and I challenge you to study them for yourself.

So if the Lord and His Disciples prayed that way, shouldn't we do that also? This was changing the way we prayed. But another revelation was making its way into our theology. Look at Matthew 8:16b. It states, "And healed all that were sick." See the word "all"? It also appears in other verses: Matthew 4:24, 8:16, 12:15; Luke 4:40, 6:19...

It says all that came to Him were healed. He never denied anyone healing. He never told them to wait for another time (although some were healed as they went). He never said they were suffering physical sickness as an example to others on how to suffer. He never told them He would not heal them because their faith was not strong enough. In fact He healed people with much faith, little faith, mother's faith, father's faith, friends' faith, master's faith and even just His faith. It doesn't say everyone was healed, but it does say all those who came to him were.

Jesus said, *"He who has seen Me has seen the Father - John 14:9,"* and that *"He (Jesus) is the image of the invisible God." - Colossians 1:15*

Jesus never put sickness or disease on anyone, so the argument that God puts diseases on His people for some divine purpose is recognized for what it really is, another lie of the enemy. Jesus only did what He saw His Father doing.

The next revelation for us was that there are instantaneous miracles, and then there are healings. There is an example in the New Testament where people were healed as they went. In fact, it was about this time that the Lord told Heidi that my healing was not going to be an instantaneous miracle, but a progressive healing over time. Of course I didn't want to hear that. I wanted a miracle now. I didn't want to be in this excruciating pain one day longer. He told her it would be this way so I would learn how to stay healthy and not "lose my healing." I think it would be good at this point to define that term. I don't believe that we actually "lose" our healing, but that if we don't do what is necessary to keep our bodies healthy and our relationship with the Lord strong, the same thing or worse can come back. In Matthew Chapter 12, Jesus says,

"When an unclean spirit goes out of a man, he goes through dry places, seeking rest, and finds none. Then he says, 'I will return to my house from which I came.' And when he comes, he finds it empty, swept, and put in order. Then he goes and takes with him seven other spirits more wicked than himself, and they enter and dwell there; and the last state of that man is worse than the first." - Matthew 12:43-45a

I believe He meant that once that unclean spirit was gone, if the man didn't fill that place in his life with the Holy Spirit, he was putting up a "VACANCY" sign and that thing would come back worse than it was before.

In John 5 Jesus heals a man from a sickness he suffered from for 38 years. Afterward He finds the man and tells him, *"See you have been made well. Sin no more, lest a worse thing come upon you."*

I have personally witnessed people who have been healed, but didn't "maintain" their healing and it came back, sometimes worse. A good example of people in the New Testament who didn't get healed instantly is found in Luke chapter 17. It is the story of the 10 lepers.

"Now it happened as He went to Jerusalem that He passed through the midst of Samaria and Galilee. Then as He entered a certain village, there met Him ten men who were lepers, who stood afar off. And they lifted up their voices and said, 'Jesus, Master, have mercy on us!'

So when He saw them, He said to them, 'Go, show yourselves to the priests*.' And so it was that <u>as they went, they were cleansed.</u>"
Luke 17:11-14

* Note: If Jesus sent them from Galilee to the priests in Jerusalem, it could have been over 60 miles and a several day journey. How far had they gotten before they noticed they were healed? This may partly explain why only one returned to thank Him.

See the words *"as they went, they were cleansed."* Jesus' authority had healed them, but they needed to be obedient and go show themselves to the priests. They all had the faith to go at His Word and as they went they noticed that they were healed. Heidi was told by the Holy Spirit that this is what was going to happen to me. I was going to be healed, like Heidi likes to say, "As I was 'wenting'."

Another example of a related principle can be found in Mark chapter 8.

"Then He came to Bethsaida; and they brought a blind man to Him, and begged Him to touch him. So He took the blind man by the hand and led him out of the town. And when He had spit on his eyes and put His hands on him, He asked him if he saw anything. And he looked up and said, "I see men like trees, walking." Then He put His hands on his eyes again and made him look up. And he was restored and saw everyone clearly." - Mark 8:22-25

Jesus prayed for the man twice. This was Jesus. Why did he have to pray twice? Was this harder than raising Lazarus from the dead? He only had to command that once. No, I believe Jesus was demonstrating a principle for us. That healing is ours and we have to see it that way. If we don't see complete healing the first time, we need to keep praying and not give up until we get what we know is ours through His sacrifice.

Jesus illustrates this principle through a parable he told to his disciples in Luke 18:

"Then He spoke a parable to them, that men always ought to pray and not lose heart, saying: 'There was in a certain city a judge who did not fear God nor regard man. Now there was a widow in that city; and she came to him, saying, 'Get justice for me from my adversary.' And he would not for a while; but afterward he said within himself, 'Though I do not fear God nor regard man, yet because this widow troubles me I will avenge her, lest by her continual coming she weary me.'

Then the Lord said, 'Hear what the unjust judge said. And shall God not avenge His own elect who cry out day and night to Him, though He bears long with them? I tell you that He will avenge them speedily. Nevertheless, when the Son of Man comes, will He really find faith on the earth?'"
Luke 18:1-8

The principle is stated in the first verse. I like to put it this way. He told them this parable so they would keep praying and not become discouraged or quit until they got their answer. He says that God will avenge (make right the situation) as we keep crying out to Him. He is equating this persistence with faith.

I believe these insights are keys. Too many times we become disheartened if we don't get our answer immediately or within a short period of time. We are not promised instantaneous answers, but He will always answer us, and in the meantime He will be there with us in the struggle.

The Lord says to us:

"When he calls on me, I will answer; I will be with him in trouble and rescue him and honor him." - Psalm 91:15, 16. TLB

As Alex Barefoot, Lead Pastor of Eastside Church in Charlotte, North Carolina likes to say, "We have been saved, we are being saved and we will be saved." Well, since salvation includes healing, we can say. "We have been healed, we are being healed and we will be healed.

NEW HOPE ARISES

Heidi

By now it was early 2008 and I heard about an outpouring of healing that was happening in Lakeland, Florida. Ignited Church, pastored by Stephen Strader, had asked a young healing evangelist by the name of Todd Bentley to come and hold meetings for his congregation. People began to be healed in the services and soon the revival was attracting people from all over the world with as many as up to 10,000 people in attendance.

Joe and I began to watch this amazing outpouring of healing and restoration on the Internet and on God TV. The preaching and miracles confirmed what we had already been reading and watching at other churches, but the numbers of people healed were staggering. Joe would ask me many times, "Do you think those healings are real?" and "Do you think I could be healed?" I wanted to take Joe to those meetings. We even had relatives who lived in the area. But Joe was in no condition to make that kind of trip. Day after day we watched in amazement and yearned to see that kind of thing happen in our lives. Then one day as we watched we heard that Todd was coming to Concord, a town no more than 30 minutes from our home. Pastors Donna and Terry Wise from Impact Church had stepped out in faith and rented Cabarrus Arena. I decided we were going no matter what.

The evening came and we decided to get there early. I put Joe into the car with a mat and a walking stick. When we got to the arena there were hundreds of people there already. They were letting people inside in batches because there was a large crowd wanting to get in and only a limited number of seats. We were some of the fortunate ones who got inside. The event center, where Todd was going to be speaking, can hold about 8,000 people with overflow seating. By the time the event started, the arena was full. Reports said that about 5,000 people were turned away and there was a traffic jam of around 2,000 cars that formed a parking lot on the highway leading to the arena. Joe lay on the floor on his mat and could not even see the stage.

Todd spoke and called for people with specific diseases to come to the stage so he could pray for them. He didn't mention Joe's condition so we waited. At the end of the meeting they formed a healing "tunnel" for people to pass through as Todd and his leaders prayed. There was no way Joe would be able to wait in that long line, so I asked someone to take a cloth and have Todd anoint it with oil so I could place it upon Joe for healing. That night many were healed, but Joe didn't see any change in his condition. He went home disappointed and it just reinforced his feeling that he was not going to be healed. It was a setback for us, but I still knew that

God is Jehovah Rapha, the Lord Our Healer, and that Joe was going to be healed. It just was not at this event.

One of the great things about the Lakeland Outpouring being televised and online was that they not only broadcast the nightly meetings from Florida, but also many different meetings and workshops that were happening during the day by other ministers. One of these ministers was a lady healing evangelist by the name of Joan Hunter. Her parents, Charles and Frances Hunter, went all over the world holding healing meetings and were known as "The Happy Hunters."

Joan had traveled and ministered with her parents for many years. Since they were getting older and not traveling much anymore, Joan had taken over that part of the ministry. When we listened to her teaching and watched how she ministered healing to people, we were amazed at the stark difference in ministry style from what we had seen. There was no theatrics or loud shouting. She just asked the person what they needed, and then with calm, but assured authority spoke to the infirmity and commanded it to do what she wanted in the name of Jesus. She didn't even close her eyes and told the sick person to keep theirs open too. "If you close your eyes, you may miss seeing your healing," she would say. I felt what she really was saying was to throw away the trappings of what you have erroneously been taught about healing and embrace what the Bible really teaches. And the results were amazing. We saw more people get healed, right there on television, when she prayed for them, than we had seen anywhere else.

Joe was very encouraged by what he saw, but he would still ask me, "Do you think that's real? Are those people really getting healed? Do you think I can be healed too?" Joan only did a few sessions at the church in Lakeland but they would replay these sessions on God TV several times a week for many weeks. It lifted his faith so much that every time it would air on the Internet I would go into the bedroom and say, "Come on, Joan is on TV again." Joe would struggle through the pain, get out of bed, walk to the massage table, lie down again and watch Joan.

One particularly bad day for Joe, and there were many, my parents came from Florida to visit us. Joe told me to apologize to them for him because he was not feeling up to seeing anyone. This was a typical occurrence many times when people would come to the house. It happened to be Labor Day and I believe the Lord directed me to email Joan that day. I had never contacted her before, so she didn't know who we were. I emailed her about Joe's condition, asked her to pray for him and even asked her to call if she could.

Within four hours of sending that email, I received a phone call from her. She said, "Hi, this is Joan Hunter." At the "Hi, this is …" I already knew who it was. She didn't even have to tell me her name because I had heard that voice from the videos so many times. I was amazed. It was a holiday and she is a very busy lady and she took time to call us! Little did I know at the time but when she received that email the Lord spoke to her. "This one is yours," He said to her, "You are going to have to walk him through his healing." She has since told us that this kind of thing only happens rarely to her and she normally lets her ministry team make the first calls. I ran into the bedroom and said, "Joe, Joan Hunter is on the phone," and handed the handset to him.

Joe

Joan, like she almost always does, asked me about my condition. She then proceeded to pray over my body and tell the pain to leave, my vertebrae to align, inflammation to go, nerves to be restored and my body to line up with the Word of God, all in the name of Jesus. "How do you feel now?" she asked. "I don't feel any different," I said disappointedly. She said, "Hmm." Then she proceeded to pray again saying very much the same thing. "How do you feel now?" she asked again. "No different," I said again, this time almost in tears. "Hmm, you should be healed," she said with conviction, "I am going to go back to the Lord on this one," she said in a perplexed voice. "In the meantime I want you to go to a church that really believes in healing," she continued, "There is a church in Concord near you by the name of Impact Church. It is pastored by a lady named Donna Wise and her husband Terry. I ministered there a few months ago and Terry was miraculously healed of neck pain. They know the power of God and believe that He heals today. Go there and I will stay in contact with you."

Believe it or not, all I could think about at that moment was her comment that this church was led by a lady pastor. In the denomination that I grew up in, senior pastors who were female were allowed, but rare. There was still this mentality that it was fine for women to be children's pastors or music pastors, but they were not encouraged to be the senior pastor over a church. God was already starting to break down the traditions that were not from Him.

Heidi

I, on the other hand was ecstatic. Joan Hunter had called us! She felt like Joe was going to be healed! She was sending us to a church where there was hope! I couldn't wait. I had been carrying this virtually alone for so long, and I needed some support from people who believed and experienced healing.

5

HEALING BEGINS

Heidi

I remembered where I had heard these pastors' names before. They were the ones who had brought Todd Bentley to North Carolina. We had been to that event and Joe had even met Terry there and talked briefly to him. People from Impact Church were volunteering there and they had been so kind and attentive to us and prayed for Joe while he was there. I looked up the church on the Internet and found out they even had Healing Rooms there. So they really did believe that God heals today. Joe asked me to go to the first service by myself and check it out. That opportunity came on a Wednesday night.

The moment I walked through the doors two men, who I had met at the Todd Bentley event, greeted me. "Hi," one said, "We were wondering what happened to you and your husband. We've been praying for you." I was impressed. The event was in June and here it was early October, plus there were so many people at that event and they still remembered us? Wow! I already liked this place. I don't remember much more about the service except that I liked the music, Pastor Donna and the people I met. I just had to get Joe there, but could he tolerate it for a whole service? One of the ushers told me that they were having a prayer service that next Saturday night. That night I got Joe up, loaded him into the car and headed off to the church. Unfortunately, that service had been canceled. Oh Joe was devastated. "Just take me home," he said in a pitiful voice.

Joe didn't think he could sit through an entire Sunday service so we didn't go that week. Interestingly enough, at that service, a man with throat cancer was healed and also a boy who was deaf in one ear had his hearing restored. The next Saturday night they were having another service and I told Joe we needed to go.

Joe

It took a lot of encouraging, but Heidi finally convinced me that there would really be a Saturday night prayer service this time. She loaded me into the car once again and we headed off to Impact Church. We walked in and Scott, the music pastor, was singing and playing the piano. Pastor Donna was out of town, but Pastor Terry was there with many other people praying and worshiping. I hardly noticed anything else that was going on because I was so focused on the music. Pastor Scott the keyboardist and Justin the drummer were the only musicians there, but I thought I had gone to Heaven. The music was so beautiful and it seemed to fill the whole room with the Presence of the Lord. I was so dry and this felt like a gentle rain on my parched soul.

For the first time in over two years, I ignored my pain, stood, lifted my hands, closed my eyes, and got swept up in worship to my Lord. For what seemed like just moments, which actually was probably over an hour, I focused solely on Him with a true sacrifice of praise. The pain was still there, and just as intense, but the Presence of the Lord was just too strong to allow the pain to stop me. When I finally opened my eyes there were only five people remaining, Heidi and I, Scott, Justin, and Pastor Terry. We apologized for staying so long and making them feel obligated to minister to us. Scott said, "I will play as long as there is someone here that wants to worship. Don't feel bad at all. It was my pleasure." I walked over to Pastor Terry and wrapped my arms around him. He is a tall man and he towered over me. He really didn't know me and I could tell he was uncomfortable by my hug, but after the initial awkwardness, he wrapped his long arms around me and began to pray for me. I am so grateful that he did. It locked me into that church for the next 7 years and formed a friendship like I had never had before.

Over the next months we would go to Impact every time the doors were open. I only missed when the pain was so bad that I was not able to get into the car. Initially, I would go to the services, sit hunched over with my head in my hands trying to manage the pain and try to wrap my head around what was being preached. The people there were wonderful and really believed God was going to heal me. They dispelled all the lies the enemy had been telling me about healing. One lady, named Lynnsey, would tell me, "You don't even have to have faith. We will have it for you. We will pick up your mat and take you to Jesus." She of course was referring to the story of the four friends who carried the lame man on his mat, tore off the roof of a house, and lowered him down through the hole to Jesus, who in turn seeing their faith healed the man completely in Luke 5:17-26. "You just keep coming up and getting prayed for until you are totally whole. You are going to be healed," she would tell me. We also showed up at the Healing Rooms every time they were open and many different people prayed for me and encouraged me to persevere for my healing.

Heidi

The group from the Healing Rooms invited us to come to a healing meeting that was being hosted at a church in High Point, North Carolina. The speaker was Randy Clark, a well known and effective healing minister. I was concerned that the trip would be too much for Joe, but I felt very strongly that we should go. After a very long and grueling trip in the rain and getting lost along the way we arrived. Gratefully the group had saved us seats because there were hundreds in attendance and the place was packed. We listened to Randy minister about the healing power of God and how we as believers have been given the command, as well as the authority, to "heal the sick, raise the dead, cast out devils, cleanse lepers and tell the people that the Kingdom of Heaven is at hand."

After the service he called his healing teams forward and asked anyone to come up to one of the team members if they wanted healing. I took Joe and headed to the front of the sanctuary. There were people everywhere standing in lines to be prayed for. Joe was having trouble standing, so I found a line and sat him down to wait. Just then I noticed that Randy was still on the stage and he only had one person who he was talking to. I said, "Come on Joe. Let's go and get prayed for by Randy Clark." Reluctantly Joe came with me.

Randy treated us like we were the only people there. He gave us his full attention for more than 30 minutes. He listened to us intently as we described what Joe was going through. Then he prayed for him. Afterward, Randy said something to us that we will never forget, "Don't look to the 'big name' healing evangelists for healing. God can use anyone to heal you. There was a time a while back when I had back issues and could hardly walk. I could not put my foot down on the floor. I could not put any pressure on it or straighten my leg without excruciating pain. I ended up going to the doctor who found I had neurological damage to my spine.

I went to a physical therapist for ninety days, six days a week. I could not walk without crutches, could not sit in a chair without exacerbating the problem, and was reduced to lying on a mat or lying in bed. Eventually, I was given two epidurals. The physical therapist told me that if they did not help, then I would probably need back surgery. I had three herniated discs and two pinched nerves, along with two forms of arthritis in my spine. The epidurals did not help.

I went to many 'big name' healing evangelists and friends who have strong healing gifts but was not healed through their prayers. Instead, I was healed through two people who are not noted for healing. My son, Josh called me and said, 'Dad I believe God wants to heal you.' Then he prayed for me. While I received partial healing at that time, my full healing only came several weeks later. An email message from a businessman in Louisiana reported that he was granted an open vision of my back, seeing the spine and the nerves going out of the spine. He also saw Jesus tell him how to pray. He acted out everything the Lord was showing him, even though he was in a church service at the time.

The next day after waking up, I discovered I was completely healed. Without knowing about that prayer, I was able to walk without crutches for the first time in ninety days, walk stairs normally, and was free from the excruciating pain I experienced when putting my left foot on the ground."

This revelation from Randy totally changed my mindset about healing. Christians have somehow left healing to the professionals. God didn't design the Church that way. If I am a believer, then God's healing power resides in me. His name is Holy Spirit. No one has any more of the Holy Spirit than anyone else. There is no big Holy Spirit for adults and little Holy Spirit for children. There is only one Holy Spirit. The only difference is how much of us the Holy Spirit has, not how much of Him we have. Jesus' command is to all who believe and we need to start operating in His authority. Then our world will know that Jesus is the Christ.

Joe

Gradually, over the course of the next year, my healing did take place. Every time there was an invitation for people to come up for healing I would go. Every time the Healing Rooms were open I was there to be prayed for. Even if there was no invitation, I would ask those who I knew really believed in praying with authority, to pray over me. We were there at the church every time the doors were open.

At first I had faith in the faith of others. Eventually my own faith in God began to strengthen as my healing began to manifest. The healing would come in plateaus. I would get a breakthrough and then I would stay there for a while. The enemy would come along and say, "That's all you are going to get." I would say, "No devil, it's not. I am going to be totally healed." Then I would proceed to speak to the pain in my back and legs and tell it to go in the name of Jesus. Then I would get another breakthrough and the whole process would happen again and again as I inched closer and closer to total healing.

Early on in this process I decided to stop seeing the doctors and started to wean myself off all my medications. None of them was really helping me anyway. I was so addicted to some of the drugs that it took me months of carving off little slivers of each pill to reduce the dosage enough to finally get completely off of them. As I did that, my brain began to heal and I was able to focus more. If anyone, including doctors, spoke anything negative over me, I would verbally "cut it off" in the name of Jesus. The Lord's thoughts about me are *"good and not evil, plans to prosper me and not to harm me, to give me a hope and a future." Jeremiah 29:11.* I was not about to let the words of men override the Word of the Lord over me.

Every time I went to Impact I would seek out Terry. He would encourage me with stories of his encounters with the Lord. He told me the story of his miraculous healing when Joan Hunter came to their church. Terry had been suffering with incredible neck pain and headaches caused by a twisted vertebrae in his neck. You could literally feel the lump on the back of his neck and he said his wife Donna could not even bear to touch it because it felt so "gross."

He was sitting in the back of the sanctuary, with pain and a headache, running the sound board when Joan was there. All of a sudden he heard her say that there was someone there with pain in their neck that was going to be healed if they would come up to the front to be prayed for. Terry immediately left the sound board and made his way to the front. "Now that's unusual," she said, "Pastors usually are reluctant to come up for prayer." "But I want to be healed," Terry said. Joan laid her hands on his neck and spoke to the pain to go, inflammation to cease and the vertebrae to line up in the name of Jesus. The pain and headache left immediately, but he could still feel the lump where the vertebrae were twisted. "Well at least the pain is gone," he thought.

He went home that night and awoke in the morning staring at the ceiling, not really thinking about anything in particular, and definitely not about healing. All of a sudden he felt something shifting in his neck. He was lying perfectly still and not moving his head at all. "I knew what was happening," he told me, "but I wasn't even praying or even thinking about my neck at the time." Just then his vertebrae popped into alignment and the lump was gone. He didn't even tell Donna at the time, but waited until she and Joan were in the car with him on their way back to church. "Feel my neck," he told Donna. She reluctantly conceded and put her hand where the lump used to be. "It's gone!" she said in surprise. And it has stayed in place ever since.

Terry told me about an event in their lives that changed the way they viewed their relationship with God. They had heard there was more of God than what they were experiencing. They decided to attend a conference that focused on the supernatural power of God. During one of the ministry times, they both went to the front to be prayed for. One of the ministers laid his hands on them and prayed over them. They both felt God's supernatural Presence like they never had before. They were so overwhelmed that neither of them said a word to each other. Finally, when they got back to their car, they turned to one other and asked, "Did you feel that?" When they compared their experience, it was exactly the same. This set them on a quest to experience all God had for them so they could share it with others and become all God designed them to be.

After this encounter Donna would get prophetic pictures as God showed her what He was doing. Terry would have prophetic dreams and then wake up, open his eyes and see what seemed to be a movie screen pulled down in front of him that finished the vision he had started in his sleep. He told me about encounters with angels and with the Lord that made me jealous for the same. At one point I wanted to start seeing God's supernatural power so badly that I asked Terry to lay hands on me and pray that the Lord would start to show me signs too. I didn't realize how quickly the Lord would answer his prayer.

GOD'S UNIVERSITY

Joe

God is so faithful and so personal. I am such a literal person and need tangible things that will keep my faith strong so that I can share them with others. Little did I know that when I asked for signs that He would answer me with literal "signs." The next Sunday, after Terry prayed that the Lord would show me signs, he and Donna invited Heidi and me to go to lunch with them. I was feeling so bad and worn out that I asked Heidi if we could just go home. She reluctantly complied, but she really needed to fellowship with other people.

While we were on our way to our house I realized her need to socialize and told her that I would just stick it out and let's just go to the restaurant. That caused her to drive to the place a different way than if we had traveled straight from our church. We passed by a large church on the way and a car pulled out in front of us. The license plate on the car was "JHVRAPHA." I stopped talking to Heidi and turned to her and said, "Do you see that plate? God is talking to us through that license plate. He is saying, "I am Jehovah Rapha, the LORD who heals you!" We were stunned. When we got to the restaurant that was all we could talk about. The Lord was confirming that He was going to heal me.

The next week Heidi was traveling in Matthews, which is an adjacent town to Charlotte. She had to stop for a red light and she thought she recognized the truck in front of her. It was the wrong color though. When she looked at the license plate it encouraged her greatly. It read "HEALD!" She couldn't wait to come home and share the news. God was again confirming His intent to heal by showing her a license plate that she interpreted as Healed!

The next day I was setting up an account for Heidi on PayPal. Before I could set up the account, the website made me type in a series of characters from a picture at the bottom of the screen. Normally it's a combination of letters and numbers or a common word. This was not. The characters I was instructed to type were "JHHVH." It reminded me of the Jewish abbreviation for the name Jehovah. Just to make sure this was not a coincidence, I tried it again. It was completely different. I figured out the chances that something like this could happen and calculated that it was 1 chance in over a billion-billion. I interpreted these 3 signs as the Lord saying, "I am Jehovah Rapha, the LORD who heals you. You are going to be healed for I am Jehovah." I would repeat this prophecy over and over to myself many times a day through the course of my healing.

License plates, electronic signs, street signs, emails, texts and other kinds of written things started appearing on a frequent basis. We never looked for them; they just kind of showed up when we needed them. Some would come to encourage us. Others showed us how God wanted us to invest some of our money. At times they would come as a direct answer to our prayers or confirmation as to what God was saying through His Word or through His messengers.

Donna Wise is a very gifted pastor and teacher. She is the most gifted, in my opinion, on the topic of what some call "Inner Healing." She and Terry own several successful professional counseling centers in North Carolina and use many of these Biblical principles with their clients when they are allowed to. Very early in our time at Impact Church we were privileged to attend one of the extended seminars they used to have. I had taught Young Married Sunday School for about 10 years and had helped many couples find their way to a healthier and a happier future. Many of the subjects she taught I had also taught, but the insights the Lord had given her were far beyond what I conveyed in my classes.

It was not surprising to learn that many Christians may put on a good front in public but in private they are totally different. What was surprising was the depth of the dysfunction. Anger, bitterness, unforgiveness, depression, loneliness, sadness, self-doubt and criticism are constant companions of so many in the church. They live inside cages of their own making and doubt that God even cares about them. Most had help getting there because of some form of abuse in their lives from parents, siblings or other family members. Later on others joined in the fray. Spouses, pastors, teachers, employers and even so called friends helped them in the making of their personal prisons.

Whether the abuse was actual or perceived, physical, mental, emotional or sexual, the bars become stronger and more plentiful. For so many there seems to be no way out.

Donna has one statement that I feel sums up how Christians can gain their freedom. "But God..." The two words appear in various forms hundreds of times in Scripture. For every excuse of why a person feels they should stay in their cage, this is the rebuttal. "I don't know how I can ever forgive my parents." "But God..." I don't know how to get out of this depression." "But God..." I don't know how to stop this critical spirit I have." "But God..."

The first class of the seminar was always a revelation of how our Heavenly Father sees us. Each one of us is His masterpiece. Each one of us is as important to Him as Jesus. He is no respecter of persons. We are all His favorites. We are children of God our Father, Who gave everything He had in the person of His Son Jesus, Who saved (sozo) us and set us free. Each of us is that important to God and each of us has a God planned destiny waiting to be discovered and walked in. It is the devil who comes to steal, kill and destroy; not God. Jesus came to give us life and give it to us more abundantly.

The rest of the seminar was filled with teaching that exposed the lies of the enemy that are contrary to this one truth. They opened the eyes of the participants to their own wrong thoughts that were keeping them imprisoned. There were many group sessions with hands on exercises that brought out each person's particular issues and helped them to find practical answers on how to overcome them. Heidi and I were so impressed, that we volunteered to be facilitators at most of those seminars from then on. We saw so many people delivered and their lives changed over those years and we are so grateful for that opportunity to learn to help others in that arena.

Heidi

A significant thing happened during one of the Inner Healing Seminars we helped with. We often wondered why the Lord said that through Joe's progressive healing he would learn how to not "lose" his healing and stay healthy. We had seen many people get miraculously healed. But, there were a few that would get the same thing back again or even something worse. The Lord was about to show us at least one reason why this happens.

In one of the seminar's breakout sessions, Joe and I had a group of all women. One of the questions that each person had to answer was, "What do you think is keeping you from your God given destiny?" After each one wrote their answer on a piece of paper, Joe asked if anyone was willing to share their answer. In a split second, one woman, we will call her Dana (not her real name), said boldly, "Oh I will." She then proceeded to say that she had been suffering for years with debilitating fibromyalgia and arthritis. She had applied for Social Security Disability, but that was still in process. She could hardly get up in the morning to take her kids to school and even housework was almost impossible. She was the sister of one of the ladies in the church and the two of them wanted to start a small business together, but because of her illness she could not do what she felt destined to do.

Dana's husband, her sister and her sister's husband had come to the seminar also, but were in other groups. Joe said, "Well then, let's just pray right now so you can be healed and get that thing out of the way. Ladies, lay your hands on her while I pray." He prayed just like we had been taught. "In the name of Jesus I speak to you fibromyalgia, GO right now! Arthritis, GO! All inflammation and pain GO! Muscles be restored. Joints go back to normal and cartilage and bone be restored in the name of Jesus." Since his faith was not quite mature yet, he hedged, "Now Dana, sometimes there are instantaneous miracles and sometimes there are progressive..." He didn't even get the word "healings" out of his mouth before she started shouting, "I'm healed, I'm healed, I'm healed!" The shock on Joe's face was priceless. God had at least confirmed one principle we had learned. It is not about how much faith we have, it is about obedience. We are responsible for the natural. The Lord is responsible for the supernatural. She ran out of the room to find her husband, sister and brother-in-law. They couldn't believe it. She was totally restored. She bent and twisted and raised her hands above her head. She jumped and shouted and let everyone know she was healed.

Joe

For the next 3 months, every time I would see Dana or her sister I would ask how she was doing. And for 3 months the report came back that she was still enjoying her healing. She was driving her children to school, doing housework and even stood on a table to clean the ceiling fan. Then one day her sister told me it all came back. "Really, the fibromyalgia and the arthritis both came back?" I asked, "What happened?" "Well you remember when she told you that she had applied for disability?" she replied, "If she had no pain she could not qualify for the disability check and she wanted that more." I was floored. I couldn't believe it. I had been on disability and gladly gave up my pain even knowing I would lose that income.

As Jesus told His disciples:
"When an unclean spirit goes out of a man, he goes through dry places, seeking rest, and finds none. Then he says, 'I will return to my house from which I came.' And when he comes, he finds it empty, swept, and put in order. Then he goes and takes with him seven other spirits more wicked than himself, and they enter and dwell there; and the last state of that man is worse than the first. So shall it also be with this wicked generation."
Matthew 12:43-45

Remember, if we don't fill that empty place that is vacated when we are healed with the mindset from the Spirit of God, then that place gets filled back up with the same lies of the enemy that got us into our situation in the first place. It opens the door for the problem to come back in even a greater measure than before. We must be ever vigilant to maintain our healing by being selflessly obedient to His Word and His plan for our lives.

BACK TO WORK

Joe

It had been a wonderful year. My pain continued to abate and my mind was healing also. I was ready to go back to work. When I started on disability, the counselor told us that over 90% of the people who get on Social Security Disability never get off. Praise God I wasn't going to be one of those. Graciously the president of the computer software company where I was an analyst said that he would give me my old job back. This was definitely an answer to prayer and a blessing from the Lord. Not many places will take a chance on someone that has been disabled for that long.

It was good for my brain to have to be stretched again. The medications and stress had caused it to have many memory "holes." I remember one time I was trying to think of the name of my uncle, the oldest of my mother's three brothers. I had grown up knowing all of their names even as a small child. Tom, Dave, and ????. I couldn't remember no matter how hard I tried. Finally I asked Heidi what his name was. "John," she said. "Oh yes. Tom, Dave and John. Wow I can't believe that was missing," I replied with a sigh. This was one "fact" among many that seemed to be behind walls in my mind. Once I was able to pull the walls down and re-establish those facts, I could remember them again. To this day I am still excavating old memories and putting them in their proper place.

Heidi

As Joe was being healed, I was also regaining my freedom. It was no longer necessary for me to be on call every hour of every day for him. I could finally have my own schedule and it was wonderful. One day Joe and I were driving somewhere in the car and we were having a discussion. Suddenly there was an uncomfortable chill in the conversation. "I feel like a wall just went up between us," he said. I felt it too, but I didn't know why it happened. As I began to think about it, the reason came to the forefront of my mind. "I guess I am angry with you for being sick for all those years and keeping me a virtual prisoner in my own home," I said. I had not thought about it until that very moment, but I realized those years had taken a severe toll on me also and I resented him for that. I needed healing as much as he did. It just was more emotional and mental than physical. With the help of the Holy Spirit I have been able to get that restoration. We must always remember that many times sickness and disease affect more than just a single person. We need to be aware that caregivers and other family members may also need healing and minister to them as well.

Joe

It was by going back to work that God reinforced two important principles in my life. One had to do with the word he spoke to Heidi about staying healthy. I had lost, over my working history, about 5½ years of working income. Three of those years were due to my disability. Retirement age was not too many years on the horizon and I felt that I had not done a good job of investing for the future. I was determined to make up for that now. Not only did I work at the software company during the day, I also worked for another computer company during my off hours. Sometimes I would work 80 to 90 hours a week total. Not that working that many hours is wrong, but my reliance on myself to assure our financial future was. As I have said before, too many people, once they are healed, go right back into things that got them there in the first place. In my case, the Lord had always taken care of us financially. Why was I to think He would not do that in the future? When the Lord showed me that I was working those extra hours out of fear and not obedience, I had to repent. "Lord," I prayed, "I trust You. You love me and You have always provided. I will not work ever again out of fear, but will always remember that You hold my future in Your hands." Now I work for one company and work a normal number of hours per week doing a job that I enjoy. I no longer fear for the future because I know the One who is Faithful.

The second principle that God reinforced was how much He loves every one of us. One day, about a year after returning to work, I was feeling a little down and just needed some comfort from the Lord, I asked God very innocently, but very sincerely, to let me know that He loved me in some tangible way. As I said in the previous chapter, the Lord often talks to me in signs. But this day I wasn't really thinking along those lines. I just wanted the Lord to let me know He loved me in an undeniable way. Of course we have the scriptures that let us know that, but I wanted something a little more personal.

That very afternoon, not more than 4 hours after that prayer, while I was leaving a store parking lot, an SUV happened to catch my eye. It had been parked about 5 cars down from my van. There was something strange about the license plate. You see, in North Carolina, most plates are 3 letters, a dash, and then 4 numbers. This plate was 8 letters with no spaces. As I looked, tears came to my eyes and a tremendous warm feeling of God's love flowed like warm honey over my entire being. Even as I am writing this, that feeling is overwhelming me again. The plate had the embossed letters, "ILUVUJOE" emblazoned on it. I just had to stop my van, pull out my cell phone and take a picture. I thought, "Just think how much God has to love me to take the only car in North Carolina with that plate, put it in that parking lot, on this day, at this time, and get me here so I can see that God, the ruler of the universe loves me. Not only does He love the world, He loves ME!"

At that moment I heard the Holy Spirit speak to my heart and say that this event wasn't only to let me know that He loves me individually and personally as His child, but He wanted me to tell this story to those I come in contact with, and let them know that He loves them the same way.

Since that time I have told this story to many people and have seen the effect it has had on their lives. Most people can't believe it until I pull out my cell phone and show them the picture, but the response is almost always the same; their eyes begin to water as they start to understand the love the Father has for them. Not just "God so loves the world" in general, but the Father loves THEM and knows THEM by name.

Some people have asked me if I am someone special that God would do this for me. I tell them that I am just as special as any other child of God, but I did one thing that most of His children don't do. I asked. I believe if someone will dare to ask, the Father will answer them also. Maybe not in a license plate, but in a way that is very unique and special to them.

I shared this story just recently with Tabitha, a young woman we know from church. You could just see the countenance on her face change when she read the words on the license plate, "ILUVUJOE." I told her that if she would ask the Father, He would show His love to her in her own special way. She asked, and the Lord answered. This girl had grown up in difficult circumstances and had a very strained relationship with her own father. One night, the same week, she had a dream. She was having a picture taken with her father. Just before the flash of the camera her father leaned over and wrapped his arms around her in a warm parental embrace. She was surprised and overwhelmed by the love she felt at that moment. She couldn't resist that love even if she wanted too. When she woke up the Lord revealed that her earthly father in the dream was symbolic of her Heavenly Father, and it was really Him embracing her and showing her how much He loves her! It was her "ILUVUTABITHA" moment and the Lord expressed it in the way it would make the most impact on her. When Tabitha told us the story, you could see the glow on her face because she knew how much her Heavenly Father loves HER!

Through my "ILUVUJOE" encounter with God, I believe I have learned something else about His love for us. God is an infinite God. Now I was taught that infinity divided by anything is always still infinity. Therefore, infinity divided by the "number of humans born since the time of creation (Over 100 billion)" is still infinity. So the Father, Who is infinite love, loves YOU infinitely. Since He loves YOU infinitely, then you truly can say He loves YOU best. YOU are His favorite. You can truthfully say that YOU are His favorite without taking anything away from anyone else. We all are His favorites.

The Lord showed this to me in a practical way when Heidi and I went to the beach with our granddaughters. We had built a large sand castle with a moat. The girls were going down to the shore with buckets, scooping up the water and running back to fill up the moat over and over again. Did I tell them to stop because by doing this, the ocean would run out of water and there wouldn't be anything left for me? Of course I didn't. We could line every person on the earth up on the seashore and they could scoop buckets of water out of the ocean as fast as they possibly could, and the ocean level wouldn't even perceptively drop. That is the love of the Father. There is more than enough for anyone and everyone. And there is certainly more than enough for YOU.

There is an old song that they used to sing in the church I grew up in.

> *"It is no secret, what God can do. What He's done for others, He'll do for you."*

I challenge you to ask the Father today to show you how much He loves YOU. Ask Him to show this to you in a way that will impact you enough that you will not forget it even in the hardest times of your life. He is faithful, able and willing to show His children how much He loves them and that every one of us is His favorite.

In fact, why don't you ask Him to do that now? Then, write this date in the margin of this book or on your calendar. See how fast the Father answers your prayer. Write us and let us know when He does and how it impacts your life.

"How precious it is, Lord, to realize that you are thinking about me constantly! I can't even count how many times a day your thoughts turn

toward me. And when I waken in the morning, you are still thinking of me!" - Psalm 139:17-18 TLB

TRAINING IN THE
MIRACULOUS

Joe

We want to relate some testimonies of the miraculous power of God. Each one, whether we were directly involved or not, taught us more about the authority we have as believers in Christ over all the power of the enemy. Every one of us can heal the sick. Every one of us can bless and not curse. Every one of us can go around and do good things and destroy the works of the devil.

One night the men from Impact Church were invited to a special men's meeting at another church. There were men there from several other churches in the area. We had a great time of eating, worshiping and teaching that night as the men joined together in unity of purpose. After the speaker was done teaching he asked if there were any men there that needed prayer for anything. Several men raised their hands. Then he asked the other men in attendance to pick a person, ask what they were in need of, and pray in faith believing that what we asked for would be accomplished. Pastor Terry and I picked the same man and asked him what he wanted prayer for. He told us that he was deaf in one ear and wanted his hearing back. I had never prayed for a deaf person that was healed so I looked to Pastor Terry for guidance. He laid hands on man's ears, I laid my hands on the man's feet and the other men laid their hands on him too. Terry began to pray that the man's deaf ear would be healed and for his hearing to return in the authority of Jesus. When he was finished praying, much to our surprise, the man said he could hear out of his ear again.

Little did we know how much of a miracle this was. The man went on to tell us that the reason he had been deaf in that ear was because he had a tumor wrapped around the bones in his middle ear that facilitate hearing. When they removed the tumor during the surgery, they had to take out the bones too. There was no way he should be hearing this well. Wow! God had not only restored his hearing, but had done a creative miracle to accomplish it.

A few weeks later we heard more of the story. The man had gone home and when he walked down the hallway he heard a noise. He asked his wife, "What is that noise I am hearing." "That's the bathroom fan," she said. After that he walked to the other end of the house and told his wife to say something so he could see if he could hear her. She didn't shout, but said something to him in a normal voice. He could hear her perfectly from that distance without a problem. Yay God!

I had always wondered what happened to that man. Was he still healed? Two years after that, Terry and I were at an outdoor worship event in the center of the city of Concord, North Carolina. They had a number of worship bands and special speakers there. A man walked up to the microphone and started to share a testimony of how God had healed his deaf ear. We recognized the testimony and the man. He was still healed, still rejoicing, and still sharing his testimony. Praise the Lord.

Heidi

During this time period, we got an email from Joan. "You need to go on this church website and watch this video," she said. The video was of a woman who was attending one of Joan's healing school services. This lady had arachnoiditis, the same disease as Joe, for 13 years. She described it this way, "It's like sliding down a razor blade into iodine." She had been prayed for by many healing evangelists, but to no avail, and had almost given up.

When she heard about Joan, she told the Lord, "All the people who have prayed for me in the past didn't even understand what I am going through. If this lady can tell me, I know You will heal me." Joan was calling out people who needed healing in their back and this woman came up for prayer. After many people were healed, Joan turned to this woman. "What do you need prayer for?" she asked. "I have excruciating pain in my lower spine. The nerves are matted together and ..." the woman began saying. But before she could continue Joan said, "And you have ..." and began to describe all of her symptoms entirely. The lady was amazed. "How did you know?" she asked. "There is a man named Joe in North Carolina who was completely healed of this very same thing and you can be healed too," Joan replied. As soon as Joan prayed, the symptoms disappeared in a moment and she went back to her church dancing and rejoicing. Her pastor was so amazed at the difference in her that he wanted to know what had happened. She was able to tell him of God's goodness and healing power. She also came back to Joan's meeting the next night to give her testimony.

When Joan Hunter would come to North Carolina, we would try to go to her meetings or healing schools. Joan's mission statement "Taking the healing power of God beyond the 4 walls of the church to the 4 corners of the earth," should be the mission of every believer, and we were hungry to learn everything we could about healing people physically, mentally, emotionally, spiritually and financially. Every time we went, we were amazed at how many people got healed in every meeting. During the schools, she taught how to pray for people through practical examples. For every area of need she would ask people to come up to the front and begin to instruct us on how to pray for that issue. Most of the time, the person would be healed or have the need met right then. Then she would have the students use that knowledge to pray for others in the class and many times we would see the same results.

Sometimes Joan would come to Charlotte to do a taping of the TV show Sid Roth's "It's Supernatural." She is one of his favorites and has been on his show more times than any other guest. We would make sure we were there to chauffeur her around, if she needed it, and attend the taping of the shows.

Many times she would have Joe give his testimony and help while she prayed for the sick. After the show was done she would stay around and pray for the studio audience and backstage personnel.

Sometimes there were so many in need of healing she would recruit us to come and pray for people too. We started to see many people we prayed for being healed right in front of our eyes. We found that there was just as much need for emotional and mental healing as there was for physical healing. We were learning to be bolder when we prayed.

Joe

I was getting so excited about all the healings we were seeing, but I wanted to see more. In my exuberance I told the Lord, "I want to see all of the people we pray for healed!" Right at that moment the story in Acts about the lame man at the Gate Beautiful who was healed by Peter and John came to my mind. Jesus must have passed by that man hundreds of times. Acts 3:2 says that he was laid at the gate daily since he was born. But Jesus didn't even reach out a hand to heal him. He had the ability to heal him, but it was not the Father's timing. That man was to be healed later by Peter and John for a specific Kingdom purpose. (Read Acts chapter 3 for the incredible outcome.)

I believe the Lord was teaching me that I would not see all of the people I pray for healed until I was able to hear Him like Jesus did while He was on the earth. Jesus healed all of the people who came to Him, and all of the people the Father sent

Him to. But God didn't direct Him to heal every person He came in contact with in every situation. I was humbled. The answer always comes back to obedience and hearing the voice of the Lord through a current and close relationship with Him.

This encounter also helped me with a challenge that I have heard people make and I didn't have an answer for. "Why," they say, "If these people who heal by faith are real, don't they go into all the hospitals and clean them out?" I believe I now know the answer. First of all, I know most of us don't hear the Father like Jesus did. Secondly, even if we did, I believe the Lord would not tell us to do something like that except in very special situations under the direction of the Holy Spirit. For example, I have heard some testimonies of missionaries overseas going into a hospital or clinic and healing everyone there and it having a profound effect on a city or a village. It served a greater Kingdom purpose.

Let's look at what Jesus did in a similar situation:

"After this there was a feast of the Jews, and Jesus went up to Jerusalem. Now there is in Jerusalem by the Sheep Gate a pool, which is called in Hebrew, Bethesda, having five porches. In these lay a great multitude of sick people, blind, lame, paralyzed, waiting for the moving of the water. For an angel went down at a certain time into the pool and stirred up the water; then whoever stepped in first, after the stirring of the water, was made well of whatever disease he had. Now a certain man was there who had an infirmity thirty-eight years. When Jesus saw him lying there, and knew that he already had been in that condition a long time, He said to him, 'Do you want to be made well?'

The sick man answered Him, 'Sir, I have no man to put me into the pool when the water is stirred up; but while I am coming, another steps down before me.'

Jesus said to him, 'Rise, take up your bed and walk' and immediately the man was made well, took up his bed, and walked." - John 5:1-9

Do you see it? This was probably the closest thing to a hospital in Jesus' day. It was like an Emergency Room. Here all the "patients" were lying around waiting to be treated. When the angel came down at a certain time and stirred the water, the first person who was able to get into the pool was healed. The rest had to just wait for the next opportunity. Jesus walks into the midst of that "hospital" and picks one man to heal him. I am assuming there were dozens or possibly over a hundred people there. Why only that <u>one</u>? It certainly was not because he was more righteous or more deserving than the rest, because later Jesus warns him to *"<u>Sin no more</u>, lest a worse thing come upon you."* It was because that man was the one the Father told Jesus to heal at that time for His own purposes. Read the rest of the story to see the outcome.

I don't want to suggest that we should just sit around twiddling our thumbs and wait for the Lord to give us somebody's name. We have done that for too long and used it as an excuse for not praying for people. We need to have the compassion of Jesus for people out there in our world and be available to pray for anyone. Then we need to ask the Lord every day to identify those He wants us to pray for. We should always be ready for Him to show His Glory through us.

"And when Jesus went out He saw a great multitude; and He was moved with compassion for them, and healed their sick." - Matthew 14:14

So now our prayer is that someday we can see every person who comes to us, and every person He identifies or sends us to, healed. We want to be so close to the Lord that we can feel His heartbeat and hear His voice clearly. To re-present Him well.

I want to note that we are specifically talking about healing here. Jesus preached the Good News of the Kingdom to everyone, and told us to do the same.

"And He said to them, 'Go into all the world and preach the gospel to every creature.'" - Mark 16:15

So you don't have to ask what God's will is when it comes to evangelism. This verse is quite clear about what His will is.

We started to minister as much outside the church as we did inside. One of my friends was having troubles financially. His wife's job provided the primary income and he stayed home to school his children. When he could, he would do handyman work, but that was sporadic at best. They needed him to be earning more income to make ends meet. I met with him and we discussed this problem. We agreed that God wanted to meet his family's financial needs and that the Lord was fully capable of finding jobs for him to do. I asked Him to trust God and pray that He would bring the jobs.

From that point on, every time I saw him I would say, "Be blessed and highly favored" and "You are God's favorite." I prayed that God would show him His goodness and faithfulness. Within a month or two he had so much business he had to find other people to help him. He did work on the home of a man whose business manages hundreds of rental properties. That man was so impressed with the quality and speed of the work, that he told him that he could keep him busy for as many hours a week as he wanted fixing his rentals. He also said he could have his pick of the jobs. Thank you Jesus!

Jesus said, "Assuredly, I say to you, whatever you bind on earth will be bound in heaven, and whatever you loose on earth will be loosed in heaven." - Matthew 18:18

We were learning that we are our Heavenly Father's children. We have the power to bless or curse. Sometimes cursing comes in the form of speaking negative things over our own lives or the lives of others. We need to choose to bless. We need to speak not what we see, but what we <u>want</u> to see, and make sure that it lines up with the Word of God. The Lord lets the rain fall on both the just and the unjust. We want, and need to be, more like Jesus.

TRAINING IN THE MIRACULOUS

D. E. A. R.

Joe

One night I had a dream. In my dream 4 large letters were standing on top of each other. The letters spelled DEAR. I knew that the letters stood for something and so I asked the Lord what that was. He said, "The D stands for Demonstrate and the A stands for Activate." Then I woke up. After I awoke I asked the Lord what the other letters stood for. He said, "Get up and get a piece of paper and something to write with and I will tell you." I jumped up and did just what He said. He told me the other letters stand for Equip and Release. He said this is how Jesus taught and this is how I want my children to be taught.

Demonstrate
Equip
Activate
Release

Here is what I have found as I have sought the Lord on the
D. E. A. R. process:

DEMONSTRATE

*"That which was from the beginning, which we have heard, which we have
seen with our eyes, which we have looked upon, and our hands have
handled, concerning the Word of life - the life was manifested, and we have
seen, and bear witness, and declare to you that eternal life which was with
the Father and was manifested to us - that which we have seen and heard
we declare to you, that you also may have fellowship with us; and truly our
fellowship is with the Father and with His Son Jesus Christ. And these
things we write to you that your joy may be full." - 1 John 1:1-4*

Jesus demonstrated what He preached to His disciples. When
He commanded that they go and heal the sick, He showed
them how to heal every kind of sickness and disease. When He
said raise the dead, they observed Him raise the dead right
before their eyes. When He said cast out devils, they saw Him
not only cast out one, but a legion of demons. When He said
cleanse the lepers, He would show them how to cleanse one or
even ten at a time. He said, when you do these works, tell the
people the Kingdom of Heaven is already here. Then He
preached that very message to the multitudes so His disciples
could see how. When they didn't understand what He was
saying, He took them aside and explained it in terms that they
could understand. The way Jesus taught was "hands on." He
could really instruct, "Do what I say <u>and</u> what I do."

I have seen pastors and other leaders in the church teach the principles of the Kingdom, but not actively demonstrate, to those who are under their care, how to live them out in their everyday lives. They preach healing, but they never demonstrate healing. They tell people to witness, but aren't witnessing outside the church. Some don't out of fear of failure, but others because they have not truly learned how themselves. Their people go out and try, but they too flounder and many fail because they have no mentor to show them.

So they feel guilty because they don't see success and eventually just come to the conclusion that the supernatural power of God either isn't for today, or if it is, it must be for the select few, the "professional ministers". And the work of true ministry, by the children of God, never gets to the people who need it the most.

The Lord was teaching me that demonstration must always be the first step in making disciples. If we can't teach people how to do something by showing it to them by example, then we need to learn how to do that. We may need to find a mentor ourselves. Or, if there is not one available, He can mentor us by the Holy Spirit alone. We need to demonstrate how to heal the sick, raise the dead, cast out devils, cleanse lepers and preach the Kingdom of Heaven is already here.

EQUIP

"And He Himself gave some to be apostles, some prophets, some evangelists, and some pastors and teachers, for the <u>equipping</u> of the saints for the work of ministry, for the edifying of the body of Christ"
Ephesians 4:11-12

Some leaders and teachers use this verse in Ephesians as an excuse for why they are not out there doing the work of ministry themselves. They believe that their job is just to equip. "We are just responsible to teach it, but the people are responsible for doing it, because they are the ones who are out there" is a declaration they use to make themselves feel better. Well if you look at the rest of these verses you will see why God calls leaders, who are mature in faith and in their demonstration of the Kingdom of God.

"Why is it that he gives us these <u>special abilities to do certain things best</u>? It is that God's people will be <u>equipped to do better work for him</u>, building up the Church, the body of Christ, to a position of strength and maturity; until finally we all believe alike about our salvation and about our Savior, God's Son, and all become full-grown in the Lord - yes, to the point of being filled full with Christ.

Then we will no longer be like children, forever changing our minds about what we believe because someone has told us something different or has cleverly lied to us and made the lie sound like the truth. Instead, we will lovingly follow the truth at all times - speaking truly, dealing truly, living truly - <u>and so become more and more in every way like Christ</u> who is the Head of his body, the Church. Under his direction, the whole body is fitted

together perfectly, and <u>each part in its own special way helps the other parts</u>,
so that the whole body is healthy and growing and full of love."
Ephesians 4:12-16 TLB

In a nutshell, the Lord wants those mentors who are good examples, to equip His children. These are people who are actively demonstrating the Kingdom of God in their area of ministry so they can equip the saints to do the same, and keep them from going off track by speaking truth and dispelling the lies of the enemy.

The Apostle James puts it this way:

"But someone will say, 'You have faith, and I have works.' Show me your
faith without your works, and I will show you my faith by my works."
James 2:18

Equipping is broken into 4 other 'E's: Exhort, Educate, Empower and Encourage.

Exhort

To exhort can mean "to call near." When we exhort, we call people to examine spiritual principles more closely to help them lead a healthier and more productive life in Christ. Many people believe that the commands of Jesus apply to their leaders or someone else who is "more qualified" but not to them. Part of the job of making disciples is to wake them up. This means calling them to re-examine the commands of Christ in light of the fact that they are qualified just because they are children of God alone. And, to let them know these really are commands and not just suggestions.

Educate

Much of the ministry of Jesus was teaching the principles of the Kingdom of God. Many times He used parables as examples of these precepts.

"And the disciples came and said to Him, 'Why do You speak to them in parables?' He answered and said to them, 'Because it has been given to you to know the mysteries of the kingdom of heaven, but to them it has not been given.'" - Matthew 13:10-11

Jesus was always eager to explain when the disciples didn't understand. He also built upon each principle with deeper knowledge as they were able to grasp the simpler concepts. He also knew that some things could only be taught by the Holy Spirit after Jesus went back to Heaven.

"These things I have spoken to you while being present with you. But the Helper, the Holy Spirit, whom the Father will send in My name, He will teach you all things, and bring to your remembrance all things that I said to you." - John 14:25-26

There was one recorded instance where the concepts were so hard to grasp, that all but His closest disciples left Him. Only the ones that realized His teaching was central to their lives remained.

"From that time many of His disciples went back and walked with Him no more. Then Jesus said to the twelve, 'Do you also want to go away?' But Simon Peter answered Him, 'Lord, to whom shall we go? You have the words of eternal life.'" - John 6:66-68

Many of these principles have been lost to the church today. People have let their experiences become their theology. If something supernatural doesn't happen when they try to apply one of the principles, they conclude that it doesn't work at all. We need to teach the things that Jesus taught as foundation. We must teach people that they need to be avid students of the Word of God. The Word of God does not return void. We need to keep believing and applying it until it does work and teach others to do the same. Every time we don't see results, we need to be like the disciples who were not afraid to ask Jesus why.

"Then the disciples came to Jesus privately and said, 'Why could we not cast it out?' So Jesus said to them, 'Because of your unbelief,' for assuredly, I say to you, if you have faith as a mustard seed, you will say to this mountain, 'Move from here to there,' and it will move; and nothing will be impossible for you." - Matthew 17:18-19

As we teach people to always pray and seek His truth, we can assure them that He will be faithful to give the answers.

"Call to Me, and I will answer you, and show you great and mighty things, which you do not know." - Jeremiah 33:3

Empower

Not only do we need to exhort and educate people, we need to make sure they have the power to get the job done. We cannot do anything without the Presence of Jesus in our lives. After Jesus went to Heaven to sit at the right hand of the Father, He provided that power to us through the Holy Spirit.

"But you shall receive power when the Holy Spirit has come upon you; and you shall be witnesses to Me in Jerusalem, and in all Judea and Samaria, and to the end of the earth." - Acts 1:8

We need to make sure those we are discipling are filled and recognize the power and Presence of the Holy Spirit in their lives and ministry. We can only do the natural. He does the supernatural.

Encourage

After we exhort, educate and empower, there is one last E that is also very important. It is encouragement. Encouragement says, "YOU CAN DO THIS!"

Here is how the Apostle Paul encouraged his disciple Timothy:

"Let no one despise your youth, but be an example to the believers in word, in conduct, in love, in spirit, in faith, in purity. Till I come, give attention to reading, to exhortation, to doctrine. Do not neglect the gift that is in you, which was given to you by prophecy with the laying on of the hands of the eldership. Meditate on these things; give yourself entirely to them, that your progress may be evident to all. Take heed to yourself and to the doctrine.

Continue in them, for in doing this you will save both yourself and those who hear you." - I Timothy 4:12-16

Many times we need to humble ourselves and let those we are mentoring know the struggles we went through to get to where we are now. In essence, "If I can do it, so can you." Too many times by putting on a good face or not sharing our challenges we discourage others. The power of our testimony can make the difference between success and failure for some. We need to let them know it is a process and they WILL get there. They need to know that WE believe in THEM. Sometimes that is all it takes.

ACTIVATE

The next step in this discipling process is to activate people. Jesus used this principle with the twelve disciples very effectively.

"And when He had called His twelve disciples to Him, He gave them power over unclean spirits, to cast them out, and to heal all kinds of sickness and all kinds of disease." Matthew 10:1-4

"And as you go, preach, saying, 'The kingdom of heaven is at hand.' Heal the sick, cleanse the lepers, raise the dead, cast out demons. Freely you have received, freely give." - Matthew 10:7-8

While he was still with them and easily accessible, He sent them into all the towns and cities He was going to visit and allowed them to practice. Later He activated the seventy like He did the twelve. He did the same thing with water baptism.

"Therefore, when the Lord knew that the Pharisees had heard that Jesus made and baptized more disciples than John (though Jesus Himself did not baptize, but His disciples)." - John 4:1-2

He gave them the opportunity to co-labor with Him while He was still there to mentor them and correct anything they were doing improperly. We need to do the same. When we see an opportunity to minister, we need to call someone we are discipling over and say, "Here, use what you have seen and heard, in the authority of Jesus, to minister to this person." I have done this many times since I learned this principle, and it is amazing the confidence it instills in people and the results it brings. Every time we do this we help people to have their own testimony of how God is using them. In order for a person to witness to others, they need to have testimonies of what God has done for and through them. When they have this, it is hard to keep silent. This was the testimony of the disciples when Jesus activated them:

"Then the seventy returned with joy, saying, 'Lord, even the demons are subject to us in Your name.'" - Luke 10:17

I like to read between the lines on this verse. What I believe they were saying was, "Jesus, we were able to do all those things you told us to do; heal the sick, raise the dead, cast out devils, cleanse lepers and tell the people that the Kingdom of

Heaven is here. But we think the most exciting thing is that the demons were <u>subject</u> to <u>US</u> in your name.

Activation had given them another testimony to share and something to remember after Jesus released them into ministry.

RELEASE

This is the final stage of the discipling process. Release comes when we feel that we have given to those who we are discipling all the training they need to be successful in fulfilling their mission. At this point we entrust them to the Spirit of God and send them off to start the D.E.A.R. process with others. That is not to say we won't be there for them if they need us, but at this point they have "graduated" to be ministers who are able to teach others themselves.

Jesus did this as He ascended into Heaven.

"And Jesus came and spoke to them, saying, 'All authority has been given to Me in heaven and on earth. Go therefore and make disciples of all the nations, baptizing them in the name of the Father and of the Son and of the Holy Spirit, teaching them to observe all things that I have commanded you; and lo, I am with you always, even to the end of the age.' Amen." - Matthew 28:18-20

When God showed me this process, I was grieved because this was not the way I was discipled or discipled others. For many years now I have looked to Heaven and said to the Lord, "D.E.A.R. me Lord! D.E.A.R me!" I was sincere, and He has been faithful to send people into my life that Demonstrated, Equipped, Activated and then Released me. Every time God shows me a new point of obedience, He is faithful to take me through D.E.A.R.

I believe we never arrive at the place where we outgrow the need to be somewhere in this process. A wise minister once said to me, "You should always have both a Paul and Timothy in your life, no matter how mature you are as a Christian. We always need a person mentoring us and we should in turn be mentoring someone else."

10

CALLED OUT

Joe

God was gracious in sending us to Impact. We had learned so much there under the ministry of Pastors Donna and Terry Wise. I remember when we first started attending the church we saw it as both a hospital and a university for us. It was not only the place and people that God used to walk us through my healing, but a school where we were exposed to principles of the Kingdom that we had never heard before. Many guest speakers came and shared what was going on in ministry all over the world. There were apostles, prophets, evangelists, pastors and teachers who were equipping us to do the work of ministry. At this time we were very involved at Impact. I was helping in the audiovisual department and Heidi was the lead pianist in the worship band. Little did we suspect but after 6½ years of schooling, God decided it was time that we graduate and be released and called us out to another place to put into practice what we had learned.

We had some friends who knew that Heidi and I loved music and especially love worshiping the Lord. They invited us to a little church for a Wednesday night worship service because they wanted us to hear the really good worship band there. I told them that I rarely ever go to other churches for services and am very loyal to my own church. They said that even though they used to go to this church, they were not currently attending there. They reassured us that they were not trying to get us to go there permanently, but for just one service. Since Impact didn't, at that time, have a Wednesday night service I reluctantly agreed.

Eastside Church was only about a mile from our home. We have lived in our current house for over 20 years and I pass that church almost every day going to work. I wondered sometimes about what kind of church it was, but never had a good reason to go in to find out.

We walked into the sanctuary just before the service. A few people who knew our friends, who had gone with us, introduced themselves. But before we had a chance to meet the pastor, the worship service began. The music was really good and you could feel the Presence of the Lord there. I was really enjoying worshiping the Lord when He spoke to me. His voice was not audible, but it was so loud in my spirit that I felt like it was. That Voice was the same One that told me to marry Heidi; the One that spoke to me in the vision I had about our first son; and the One that told me ILUVUJOE. I knew it was Him.

"I want you to come to this church and serve this pastor," the Lord said. I felt an implied, "Will you do this?" even though it was not said. Because I knew it was His voice, my spirit leaped up within me and I said, "YES" even before I had a chance to think out what that would mean. Now I am not one to jump at anything. I am a person that doesn't like change. "For how long do you want me to do that, Lord?" I asked. "For a season," He said. "How long is that?" I asked. "I'm not going to tell you that yet," He replied.

I made an appointment with Alex Barefoot, the Lead Pastor of the church. I didn't even know what he or the church believed. I wanted to sit down and understand this man the Lord told me to serve. We didn't agree on everything, few people do, but I had an immediate affinity for him as a brother and I loved His passion and dedication to the Lord and His work. I told Pastor Alex what the Lord had spoken to me. I interpreted the word "serve" to mean to help him, pray for him, encourage him and exhort Him. The Lord also warned me to do exactly what He had spoken to me and to especially not seek any positions of leadership at Eastside. I was there as a servant.

I knew I had to be obedient to the Lord. I told Pastor Donna and Terry what had happened and they were gracious to release me for however long the Lord needed me. That next Sunday I was part of the congregation of Eastside Church.

Heidi

Joe told me what the Lord had spoken to him that evening. I really didn't know what to make of it. The Lord had asked Joe, but He had not mentioned what I was to do. I was very involved at Impact and felt like that was where I was supposed to stay at that time. Besides, the Lord had not told Joe how long he was going to be at Eastside. We had always gone to the same church, but Joe said I should stay at Impact if that is what the Lord was telling me. He just knew he had to be obedient to what God had asked of him. I thought he would "get it out of his system" in a month or so. Joe never pressured me to leave Impact. He did ask that I would come to Eastside for a few events and some Wednesday night services when I could. He missed worshiping together as much as I did.

We attended a new-comers dinner at Eastside together. After the dinner, each of the pastors and leaders of the church told something about themselves and their history at Eastside. One particular thing impressed me. It was the passion of the young leadership there. Even though Pastor Alex was near our age, he had amassed a group of leaders who were much younger. They were in their 20s and 30s. The church itself was full of young people. They had been praying to the Lord to send older, more mature Christians to help mentor the young people of the church. God was answering those prayers and we heard stories from many people about how God brought them, in His mysterious ways, to the church.

Joe

After that meeting I was talking to a person who we knew from Impact, but lives near us. She had never gone to Eastside and knew nothing about it, although, like us, had passed it often. One day when she and her husband were driving by Eastside, the Lord spoke to her. "There are young people in that church who are praying for Me to send them mature mentors."

HEALED!

"The effective, fervent prayer of a righteous man avails much."
James 5:16b

I began to pray for Pastor Alex almost every day. He usually is
the first person in my prayer times. I pray for the Lord to bless
him with wisdom on how to lead; health and strength in his
physical body; dreams, visions, words of knowledge and
prophecy from the Spirit; and finances to meet his every need. I
also pray for the people of the church, and especially those who
are designated as leaders, and those who don't have a title but
are leading by example. I pray for the church to become a
lighthouse in the city, state, nation and the world. I also pray
that God will bring the finances needed for the church to
achieve its destiny.

God was giving me a love not only for Pastor Alex, but the
leaders and people of Eastside Church. I began loving on
them, asking them about themselves and finding out what they
needed from the Lord. As I did this I was able to pray more
specific prayers for them and encourage them to seek the Lord
for their requests because He wanted to answer them. I would
tell them that each of them is God's favorite, because God had
revealed that to me.

One of my best analogies for how much He loves us came
from being a young father to my first son. Sometimes I would
watch him sleeping in his crib, just waiting for him to wake up.
When he opened his eyes I would get so excited and say
something like, "Hey Joey, good morning, so what are we going
to do today together?" To me that's how I view the Father with

each one of us. Like the Lord showed me, since He is infinite, He has infinite time, love and resources for each of His children. He treats every one of us like we are the only child He has.

It had been a few months since the Lord had called me to Eastside. I was seeing people healed and lives being restored in the church. I started to realize that the reason the Lord had sent me there was not only for me to minister, but also that the Lord was beginning a new phase of D.E.A.R. in my life. I was learning by serving and being obedient to His call. Since Heidi was still quite involved at Impact Church in the music ministry, and I didn't like that we were going to two different churches, I began to ask the Lord how long the "season" at Eastside was going to be. "Settle in, you will be there for a while," He answered. "Ok, Lord," I said. Now I just had to tell Heidi.

Heidi

I really thought that Joe was only going to be at Eastside for a couple of months at best. I told him that I felt like I should continue ministering on the worship team at Impact until the Lord allowed him to return. What I didn't tell him was that the Lord had started dealing with my heart also. He started telling me that my time at Impact was coming to an end and I was to join Joe at Eastside. He said that Joe and I needed to serve together, that I needed to spend more time with my grandchildren, and that my passion had begun to wane in leading worship and it was no longer going to be at the forefront where it had been for the last two to three decades.

I, like Joe, am a very loyal person. I felt if I left now, I would really hurt the worship ministry at Impact and I grieved over that. While I continued to be loyal at Impact, the Lord started to ask me when I was going to be obedient and answer His call. I realize now that it was an unrecognized "trust" issue in my life. I had become very comfortable there and was afraid to venture into the unknown.

When Joe finally informed me that God had told him that he would be there for a while, it confirmed what the Lord was saying to me. I was very reluctant, but I decided I had to be obedient. I informed Pastor Donna what the Lord had told me, received her blessing, and started attending Eastside with Joe. The Lord was about to teach both of us more about ourselves, what it really means to be a servant and the blessings that true obedience brings.

CALLED OUT

11

THE POWER OF TESTIMONY

Joe

We knew testimonies were powerful faith builders, but we didn't know how prolific they really could be. This was a lesson we were about to learn. We see in the New Testament how testimonies of healing brought people from all around to Jesus and they were healed. After the woman with the issue of blood was healed by touching the hem of His garment, they would lay people in the streets in the path of Jesus so that they could touch His hem and be healed. The testimonies of the miracles performed by Peter were so prevalent that they would lay people in the streets so that His shadow would pass over them and be healed. The testimonies of miracles performed by Paul were so powerful that they would only have to take cloths from his body to the sick and they would be healed.

I knew what testimonies did for me. Every time I would see or hear about someone being healed, especially from something similar to what I was suffering with, my faith would rise up and say, "Maybe that was real. Maybe you can be healed too!"

Without testimonies, I don't believe I would be alive today. I have watched people's faces, as I have related the testimonies of what God has done for me, light up in faith, and have even seen them healed as they believed healing was theirs also. I personally try to always tell people a testimony of an answer to prayer for a situation related to theirs, before I pray for them.

A minister once told me, "If you don't have your own testimony, pull on someone else's testimony until God gives you your own." So, if I don't have a testimony of my own of God meeting someone's need in a certain area, I use one from someone reliable that I know. A testimony says if the Lord did it once for one person, then He can do it again for you. It creates an atmosphere of faith where God can move mightily.

Let me give an example of how testimonies are prolific as they build on each other.

One day Eric, a brother in the Lord and I were putting up signs in front of Eastside Church. He was up on a ladder and hitting a piece of wood with a sledgehammer to pound sign posts into the hard North Carolina red clay. After he had been doing that for quite a while, he stopped and began to try to zip-tie a sign onto the posts. All of a sudden, he grabbed his finger and cried out, "Man that really hurts." The trauma of the sledgehammer hitting the wood had caused incredible nerve pain in that finger. Without so much as a thought I said, "Give me that finger," and I grabbed it in my hand as he held it down to me. "Finger, you be healed right now in the name of Jesus. We don't have time for this. We are trying to do some work for the Lord here. Nerve pain, go! Inflammation, go! Be restored in the name of Jesus!" I said in a normal, but authoritative voice.

As I let go of his finger, he said, "Thank you." When he began to reach back up to the sign he stopped, stared wide-eyed at his finger, and said in an amazed voice, "IT'S GONE. THE PAIN IS GONE!" I was almost as surprised as he was, but we both rejoiced and finished the work.

A few days later I was paying for groceries and talking to the lady cashier. It was very interesting because even though the store was busy, no one was in line behind me. (The Lord does this a lot for me when He wants to give me time to minister to someone.) As I began to tell her about Eric's finger healing, and a little about my own testimony, I noticed that the person who was bagging for me was listening intently too. The cashier looked at me and said, "That is amazing. Will you pray for my husband?" "What is wrong with him?" I inquired. "He has cancer," she answered. "I will do better than that. Are you a Christian?" I asked. She was, so I continued, "I am going to pray over your hands. After I do that I want you to lay your hands on your husband every chance you get and tell that cancer to go in the name of Jesus. It doesn't belong there and you have the authority to command it to go as a child of God." I prayed for her hands right there at the counter. I had no sooner finished praying when people started coming into her line.

When I saw her a month later I asked, "Are you doing what I asked you to do?" "Yes, I most certainly am," she replied. "How is he doing?" I questioned. "He's quite well. He's out fishing today!" she said with a smile on her face. About a month after that I saw her again at the store. "How's your husband doing now?" I asked. She smiled even bigger than the last time. "He is cancer free!" she exclaimed.

I was sharing these testimonies with my church family also. One night after service, Kristen, the wife of one of the men in the church, was telling me how every time her husband went out of town on business he told her to be careful while he was away. He had told me before in other conversations that she was accident prone. I went out to their car and said, "Instead of saying that to your wife, you should speak blessing over her and your family and pray for her while you are away." About two days later he texted me and told me he needed to tell me a testimony. "My wife has been dealing with severe shoulder pain for almost a year now," he said. "She could not even raise her arm above her head and definitely could not lift up anything heavy at all," he continued. "Today I laid my hand on her and prayed a simple prayer of healing for her shoulder.

I went into my home office and very shortly after that I heard her calling to me. As I looked into the kitchen to find her I could see that she was holding one of our children in the arm with the good shoulder and was waving the other arm around. 'Look honey,' she said, 'No pain. And look what else I can do.' She took some heavy bowls, lifted them above her head and placed them into the cabinet," he said excitedly. To this day she has not had that shoulder issue again.

Heidi

When we went down to Texas for some ministry classes, we met many other students from all over the world. We made sure that each one we met knew of Joe's healing and we also encouraged them with these more recent testimonies too. As we were sharing, one lady said that she had the same issue with her shoulder that the woman at our church had. She asked if we would pray for it. Since Joe tries to activate people in healing, he turned to her husband and said, "You lay your hand on her shoulder and pray and we will lay our hands on yours and agree." After the man prayed, his wife moved her shoulder around and said that the pain was gone. It was still a little sore, but we had been taught by Joan that when the pain is gone, the soreness sometimes just needs to be "worked out" as things get back to normal.

Later the same day we were in line to pick up some materials for our class. We were telling the lady in front of us these testimonies. She said before she came for ordination she was moving some racks of clothing in her store and had hurt her arm. It was in pain at that very moment. We offered to pray for her right there. After we prayed we asked how her arm was feeling. She said it was still painful, but we encouraged her to keep speaking to her arm and telling it to line up with the Word of the Lord. About 30 minutes later we were in one of the services worshiping. She was about 15 feet from us. All of a sudden she turned to us and gave us a thumbs up. The pain was gone. She had been healed. Hallelujah!

This is just one example of the power of testimonies. This powerful line of testimonies lives on as we hear reports of people continuing to be healed as they realize, through these stories, that God is still healing through His people today and that He wants to heal them. The important thing to note is that a testimony, even if it is not your own, can activate faith in both you and the person you are praying for. It also becomes something you can go back to and reflect on when the enemy tries to bring doubt or when you go through a time when healing seems elusive.

I want to relate one more story that exemplifies another healing principle. Anita, a lady in our church, had terrible, debilitating pain in her elbow because of a detached tendon. She had two surgeries to reattach it, but it would inflame and detach again. After her third surgery she was still in a tremendous amount of pain, had limited range of motion and it looked like the tendon was getting ready to detach again. She sent an email to the church that things were not right with her arm and that the pain was off the charts and asked for prayer. I was very upset because we and others had prayed for her many times with seemingly no results.

I knew that I would see her that night and wanted to encourage her and pray for her again. I saw her about four minutes before the service began and said, "I am mad!" She knew I was talking about the fact that she was still dealing with pain and replied, "Me too!" I told her the devil is a liar and that it is God's will for her to be healed. "It's not a matter of if you are going to be healed, but when," I declared. I wanted to pray for her right then, but the service was starting.

During worship, Christine, one of our worship leaders, stopped and in tears told the congregation that she was not supposed to sing the song she was scheduled for that night. The Lord was present and it was a powerful moment as she related that He was teaching her a lesson about her attitude toward worship and felt that one of the other singers should just do the next song. When the worship concluded, Christine sat down beside Anita. At the end of the service Pastor Alex had the congregation stand and hold hands for a benediction prayer. Anita tried to keep anyone from touching her arm but Christine grabbed her hand anyway. As soon as she touched Anita's hand, they both felt something.

Christine said she could feel the power of the Holy Spirit "release" from her and Anita described it as something like a lightning bolt surge through her arm. They looked at each other in surprise and Christine exclaimed, "Did you feel that?" Anita replied excitedly, "How could I not?" At that moment Anita realized her pain was totally gone and it has never come back! They were not even praying for healing, but she was healed anyway. Anita says that she wasn't even mentally "there" for the service or even thinking about healing, but she was healed anyway. Christine told us, "Afterwards, I thanked God for healing Anita and couldn't help but feel that God can use anyone, at any time, for any reason He chooses."

Yes, many times God heals just because He can. He heals us because He loves us and it is His desire that we be whole. I believe He let Christine be a part of the miracle because of her passion for the Lord and her obedience and humility in the worship service.

This incident created a testimony of healing. A few weeks later Christine saw Andrew limping in the parking lot. "What is wrong with your foot?" she asked. "Oh, it has been hurting me for a while," he said. Many of us had prayed for Andrew's foot, but it had not been healed. "Let me pray for it," Christine said. After she prayed, Andrew no longer limped. The pain was gone.

Testimonies are powerful. They create a culture of faith for miracles, healing and restoration. In that atmosphere people really believe they can heal and be healed. But there is also one more giant benefit of the power of testimony. It makes witnessing easy.

12

YOU SHALL BE
WITNESSES

Joe

I remember one Christian teacher talking about evangelism.
"Some win the lost at any cost. I teach the found while they're
still around," he said. He was a teacher and I believe he felt
witnessing was hard and since the Lord had given him a
teaching gift he could just ignore the evangelism part. I now
know this is not correct theology. Witnessing is not only a vital
part of the Christian life; it is a command from the Lord.

*"And he said unto them, 'Go into all the world, and preach the gospel to
every creature.'" - Mark 16:15*

If I went to court to be a witness of a crime and had not seen
it, the lawyer wouldn't call me to testify. I was not really a
witness. I believe the term "witnessing" in the church has
taken on a different meaning than originally intended. When
Peter and John were told to stop speaking about Jesus, this is
what happened:

"So they called them and commanded them not to speak at all nor teach in the name of Jesus. But Peter and John answered and said to them, 'Whether it is right in the sight of God to listen to you more than to God, you judge. For we cannot but speak the things which we have <u>seen and heard</u>.'" - Acts 4:18-20

They had "SEEN and HEARD!" They had witnessed something and they couldn't help themselves. They had experienced God and everyone had to know.

John puts it this way:

"That which was from the beginning, which we have heard, which we have seen with our eyes, which we have looked upon, and our hands have handled, concerning the Word of life - life was manifested, and we have seen, and bear witness, and declare to you that eternal life which was with the Father and was manifested to us- that which we have seen and heard we declare to you, that you also may have fellowship with us; and truly our fellowship is with the Father and with His Son Jesus Christ. And these things we write to you that your joy may be full." - 1 John 1:1-4

They had seen Jesus. They had heard him and touched Him. They had experienced the Messiah, the Son of God, who brought them eternal life. They were compelled as witnesses of this amazing truth to tell everyone so they could experience Him too. This is what true witnessing is.

Before I understood this, witnessing was hard for me. One reason was that I had a misconception of what witnessing really was all about. For me, witnessing was picking out a neighborhood and going door to door with a Bible in hand telling them what it said about the Lord and trying to get them saved. I could talk to people about God if they were already Christians, or those people I knew very well, but not complete strangers. I felt like I was bothering them or getting into their personal space.

That all changed when I realized it wasn't just about what the Bible said or someone else told me. I had my own testimonies. I would tell anybody and everybody who would listen, Christians or those who were not yet Christians. I could witness to them because I had experienced things that the Lord had done in my own life that I felt were so wonderful everyone would want to hear.

If they just knew how awesome God is and what He had done for us, then they would want to know Him too. If I told them that they were His favorite children too and He wants to bless them like He blesses me, they would be so excited. I was not bothering them; I was informing them about something I knew about by firsthand experience. It was not like I had to tell them so I got Christian-points or something. They NEEDED to know.

I make sure that the people closest to me know my testimonies. I tell my family, my friends, co-workers, and especially those at my church. I tell my testimonies to the cashiers and workers at the store. I tell them to people I meet when I'm out walking. I make sure I tell everyone to be blessed as a parting word. If given the chance, I pray for their needs and many times we see the answers to those prayers.

My testimonies usually bring a smile to a face or a look of amazement. When I tell them the story of "ILUVUJOE" it brings tears to the eyes of many and a new hope that God loves them specially too. If I ask someone if I can pray for them, very few ever say no. Most are appreciative that you care. Many are amazed that you're going to pray for them right then and there. I try to treat people like Jesus would treat them. I try to be kind and caring. I give them a smile and always give them my full attention. The way Christians have presented Christ in the past has given Him a bad rap. It is my responsibility to re-present Jesus to them. The Holy Spirit in us will do that if we will just let Him. This is what witnessing is all about.

13

ORDAINED

Heidi

Joan had been asking us to become ordained under her ministry. She knew we had a powerful testimony and felt like we had a call on our lives in the area of healing. She had also been encouraging us to write a book about it to help others. We appreciated her belief in us, but we were not sure what God had in store. Every time we would assist her either at her healing schools or just praying for people at the "It's Supernatural" show tapings, we enjoyed ministering to people and seeing them healed and restored physically, mentally, emotionally, spiritually and financially. We had done a lot of the preparation for ordination, but didn't feel the urgency.

One day we received a letter in the mail again informing us about the opportunity to become ordained in Joan Hunter Ministries (JHM). The date for the ordination was about a month away. Joe was showing it to me when he felt the Lord say to him, "Now is the time." And that's all He said. He didn't give an explanation as to why or what He was going to do with us. Just, "Now is the time." I was surprised, but I have always trusted that when Joe says he has heard the Lord, he has.

Joe

I knew that Voice and I knew it was God. The timing was not convenient, but many things the Lord asks of us don't come at convenient times. There were a lot of details to handle. We only had two days to the deadline of getting our paperwork in. Some of it involved getting letters of recommendation from our pastors and those who knew us well. We had to get plane tickets and hotel reservations. Most of all, there were prerequisites that we had to finish. We had read most of the books and watched the teaching videos, but it had been a long time. We wanted to study them all over again to make sure we knew all the material. Fortunately, we had scheduled a 10 day vacation at the beach that would end 10 days before we had to leave for Texas. Most of that time was used finishing the prerequisites before the ordination classes.

If we had waited even another day it might have been too late to get everything together. It all worked out by the grace of God and we were on a flight to Texas to go to the final classes and become ordained ministers under JHM. Even though we had been to so many different events with Joan, this one was exceptional. We were now making our calling public. During our time there we saw many amazing miracles and healings.

When we walked into the JHM facility there were a lot of people there. Some were those who were going to be ordained, some that had already been ordained, and some were JHM staff and volunteers. Most of them were women, and that was great, but I wanted at least one other man that I could connect with. I asked the Lord, "You brought me down here for Your purposes. Please let me find a brother in the Lord that you want me to bond with." At that moment I saw a tall man standing in the crowd of people in the worship service. I felt the Spirit say, "Him." That evening when Heidi and I were coming back from our hotel, I spotted the same man in the parking lot getting something out of his car. I walked over and introduced myself. His name was Jeff and his wife's name was Kim. It was a divine connection for both Heidi and I and we had a great time as they were both becoming ordained too.

As I said at the beginning, it was Jeff who not only encouraged me to write this book, but had the experience and knowhow to help me get it into print. I believe if God gives us a dream, He will also give us the resources we need to see it come to fruition. I know now that one of reasons the Lord told me, "Now is the time," is that He knew Jeff and Kim were going to be there and He created this divine appointment.

It is my prayer that this book has been a divine appointment for you and that you will see that you are God's favorite and He has a destiny for you. There is nothing that can stand in your way if you pursue Him with all of your heart. He is just waiting for you to recognize it.

ORDAINED

14

AND THE JOURNEY CONTINUES

The story of our journey is still not finished. We continue to see miracles and healings. Every day the Lord teaches us new principles that we didn't know or had ignored in the past. Our pursuit of His Presence gets stronger as time goes on. We have learned to "seek His Face and not His Hands." Our mission has become clearer and our faith becomes surer. As we share our testimonies, people are being encouraged and responding to the Lord. This is a sure thing, "A man with an experience is not at the mercy of a man with an argument." People are becoming free from the chains of the enemy. The fear, lies and insecurity that shackled them are falling off.

We only wish we had learned these things earlier in life, but we are encouraged that it is still not too late. The Lord told the Messiah in Psalm 2:8, *"Ask of Me, and I will give You the nations for Your inheritance, and the ends of the earth for Your possession."* We are determined to make an impact on nations for Him.

Will you join us and those that came before us and those who will come after us in taking up that call? We hope that this

119

book, this testimony of the journey to healing and beyond, will help you along on your journey to achieve the destiny that the Lord envisioned for you before the beginning of the world.

If you are reading this book and have not made a decision to make Jesus Christ the Lord of your life, or have drifted away from Him and need to recommit your life to Him, then I ask you to consider doing that right now. You don't have to be sitting in a church or have someone pray for you. Just say something like, "Jesus, I have been living life my own way. I have not been fulfilled doing that. I recognize that I need a relationship with You as Lord over my life. I realize that I have done wrong things against You, myself and others and that makes me a sinner and separated from You. I am asking you to be my Savior and my Lord and to forgive me of all my sins. I thank You for dying on the cross to do that for me and giving me a new life. I commit to reading Your Word and conversing with you every day in prayer. From now on I am Yours. Thank You Jesus!"

If you have made a commitment to the Lord just now, please email us at info@tritality.com and let us know. We want to rejoice with you. Find a church that believes the full gospel to attend and to be discipled. If you need help with that let us know.

And to all of you we speak this blessing:
"The Lord bless you and keep you; The Lord make His face shine upon you, and be gracious to you; The Lord lift up His countenance upon you, and give you peace." - *Numbers 6:24-26*

Signs and Testimonies

"But without faith it is impossible to please Him, for he who comes to God must believe that He is, and that He is a rewarder of those who diligently seek Him." - Hebrews 11:6

Joe

I am writing this bonus chapter to demonstrate the power of God in our lives. These are signs and testimonies that didn't necessarily fit in the body of this book, but are important to include in order to build up your faith. The power of testimony cannot be underestimated in our lives. If any of these resonate with you, then allow that to activate the faith the Lord has given to you to believe for the same and more.

Make It So

I was driving to work one morning asking God to be in His Presence and I saw a license plate that read "MAKE IT SO". I believe the Lord was telling me that His Presence is always there and if I wanted to be in it, I had to just "make it so" in my own life. Just live in what He has already provided.

Why Is That?

I was driving to work one day on the freeway. I was praying "Thank You Lord for being in Your Presence" and trying to have an attitude of "making it so" in my life. A car drove up just in front of the left side of my van with a license plate that read "Y-IS-THAT?" I pondered what it meant and spoke out loud, "Because I have stopped believing that I have to ask God for His Presence when He is already with me." God is so awesome!

God Is Good

I was in my van on the freeway driving to work and praying to see more of the power of God in my life. A car drove up on my left side and slowed down just enough ahead of me to read the license plate. It read "GODSGUD" and then it sped off. I believe the Lord was telling me that He is good and I will see His power in my life because that is His perfect will for His children.

Phone Interview

A young lady was visiting from another state where she was trying to get a job. While she was here, she got a call on her cell phone to come in for a personal interview. After she informed them that she could not get back in time, they told her that without being there to interview in their office in person she would not be considered for the job. She came to the front of the church for prayer on this matter. Afterward, when she walked to the back of the sanctuary, she came to me and told me her story. I placed my hand on her head and while I was praying I heard the prophetic words "phone interview." Fifteen minutes later she called me on my phone and told me that the people had called her back and asked her if she could do a phone interview instead. God had changed their heart!

I Love You

My daughter-in-law, Amanda, visited Impact Church for a special service. She was grieving over the loss of their baby through a miscarriage. I felt in my spirit that the Lord was saying to her "I love you Amanda" and He wanted to put His arms around her. After the conclusion of the service a woman named Elena came up to her and said, "I don't know you, but I have been struggling for 20 minutes with a word for you from the Lord. God says Jesus loves you and I am supposed to put my arms around you and hold you" which she proceeded to do. God cares about us and wants to comfort us more than we can imagine.

One Year Baby

Heidi helped Amanda move to Texas to join our son Joey who had gotten a job there. While they were in the area they decided to visit Joan Hunter at her ministry offices. Because of Amanda's desire to have children they asked Joan to pray for her. While Joan was praying she prophesied that Amanda would have a baby within the year. Our first grandchild, Grace, was born approximately 11 months later! The Lord will give us the desires of our heart if we trust Him. Thank you Jesus!

The Master's Key

One morning I had a dream at 5:55am. I dreamed that I was working in a hospital as an intern. I didn't see any patients, but I was interacting with the rest of the staff. I found myself in a basement room of the facility that looked like it had been dug out from a cave. The room was filled with rings of old looking keys that I knew opened individual locks to patient rooms in the hospital. Then I spotted one lone green key. All the rest were silver or brass colored. I turned to a person who had come downstairs with me and I said, "See this key? This is the Master Key." At that moment, I woke up.

I believe the interpretation of the dream is this: There are many people who are out there and are sick and hurting physically, mentally and emotionally and need to be set free. There are many different keys that the world offers, but we have been given the Master's key. He is the giver of life, (the GREEN key), and He is offering it to us to use it to free everyone we come in contact with.

Stop the Rain

This is really cool. It was supposed to rain on a particular day and my grass was getting very long because I was waiting for the new grass to come in after we had re-seeded. The rain clouds were thick as I started mowing. I was worshiping in song but it began to sprinkle. I don't like to cut wet grass and I was starting to feel soggy myself. At that moment I thought about Jesus commanding the wind and the waves and they obeyed. I looked up and said, "Lord, if it is not going to affect some master atmospheric plan, I'm going to do this," I said, "In the name of Jesus, I command the rain to stop until I get done cutting this grass." It stopped! I kept worshiping. About 5 minutes later it started to sprinkle again. I said again, "Clouds, you need to stop raining until I get this grass cut." It stopped again and it didn't rain the rest of the day!" I woke up the next morning and the ground was soaked with rain. Most people would probably think that this was coincidence. I choose to believe it was cooperation. Praise the Lord He cares about the little things too!

"For the earnest expectation of the creation eagerly waits for the revealing of the sons of God." - Romans 8:19

Healing Rain

I went to an Eastside Church men's retreat one weekend. There were over 50 men in attendance and most of them came back changed with a greater understanding of their value and identity in the Kingdom. One man I met, named Rich, told me that he had burst his left eardrum in a scuba diving accident years before. The eardrum had never healed back together again and he had very little hearing and constant pain and buzzing in that ear especially when things got quiet.

One night at the retreat, while we were in the hayloft of an old barn with a tin roof, we were praying over each other that God would place His mantle upon each one of us. I asked Rich if I could pray for his ear. As I prayed the sky seemed to break open and the rain came down in torrents. The sound was so loud on the tin roof that we could hardly hear each other praying. As soon as we were done praying, it stopped, followed by quiet. Rich looked at me and said, "I am speechless," which is very unusual for Rich, and he stayed that way for a long time.

Later I found out that not only was the pain gone and the buzzing gone, but that God had also done a deep work in his life. An issue that had happened when he was in the military, that he thought he had forgiven himself for, was healed in his heart. He was free and his face showed it. Tears flowed from his eyes. "I don't normally cry," He said, "You have seen more tears today than my wife has ever seen." To him this was a greater miracle than the healing of his ear.

Later on that night Rich also told us about lower back problems that he had been suffering with. He said that when it rains he has numbness and pain in his legs and his muscles get so weak he can hardly walk. Brannon, our Care Pastor, and I prayed for him. The next day it was raining heavily. When I asked how he was doing he said his legs were doing great. "Normally," he said, "My legs would be so bad I would have trouble walking if it was raining like this."

Two months later, Rich excitedly approached me after one of the church services. He was sitting beside his wife during worship and he actually started to hear her with the ear that had been healed. During the next two months his hearing got better and better. He decided to make an appointment with the doctor that he has been going to for years, and who is familiar with his injury, to have it checked out. When Rich told him the testimony of how he was healed, the doctor was skeptical until he looked into his ear canal. God had done a restorative miracle. The doctor found that the eardrum had completely grown back together and there was just minimal scar tissue left. He was amazed. Rich says, "I think I can hear out of that ear better than the other one!" Thank you Jesus!

Bless Them Lord

A young man, Jason, and his wife came to me one Sunday for prayer. I asked what they wanted from the Lord. They said they were having some financial problems and wanted me to pray that God would bless them. I put my arms around both of them and prayed, "Lord, I ask that You bless them financially in every way. That they will get checks in the mail, lost things found, inheritances that they didn't know they had, and people saying, 'I don't know why I am doing this for them but I want to bless them.'"

That next Wednesday night I was running the video camera in the back of the church. I was praying and asking the Lord to see more of His Glory which is His Character and Nature being manifested on the earth. At that very moment I received a text from Jason forwarded through another man in the service. It said, "If Joe is there, if you don't mind, tell him the prayer he said over me Sunday about someone giving me extra money was answered." God had answered my prayer to see more of His Glory through this brother's testimony. I pray and bless people in the natural and the Lord does the supernatural.

That next Sunday Jason told me the details of the story. He had done some work for a person at that man's house. When it came time for payment, the man asked him if he wanted cash or a check because if it was cash he would have to go to the bank. Jason told him that either was fine. The man gave him a check. Jason took it, folded it up, but waited until he got home to look at it. When he did open it up to look, the check was made out for <u>more</u> than what he had asked for. When does that ever happen? Praise God, it does when He is involved!

About a week later the Lord answered the prayer of blessing again. Jason got an unexpected raise at his job. God just continues to multiply the blessings.

Spinal Adjustment in the Night

A woman came to visit. After Heidi and I told her some testimonies of the healings we had seen, I asked if she would let Heidi and I pray for her. She had problems with her neck, spine, knees and many other things. After we laid hands on her and prayed, she was beaming. She moved her neck in positions she couldn't beforehand without pain and should have been impossible because she had several fused vertebrae in her neck.

She walked several steps, stopped moving and cried, "My back feels real hot where you prayed." "That's good," Heidi told her smiling, "That is the power of God." The woman went to bed that night and as she laid there with pain in her spine she felt a pop in her back. Some of the pain was going away. Then another pop with less pain followed by more pops and less and less pain. By the time God did the supernatural chiropractic adjustment on the vertebrae of her spine and put them back in place, her back pain was all gone. The next morning she excitedly came running down the stairs to tell us what the Lord had done.

Calf Injury Healed

Eric was playing basketball with some friends. All of a sudden he looked behind him because it felt like someone threw a fastball and hit him in the back of his lower leg. The pain was excruciating, but there was no baseball and no one had hit him.

That night he called his supervisor and told him what had happened. "I'm a runner," the supervisor said, "and from what you described to me, that's a torn calf muscle. You will be out for several weeks." The next day he went limping into work and had an awful time trying to climb the stairs to a meeting he had to attend. "What happened to you?" they asked. He told them about the injury and how it happened.

Eric called me and asked me to pray, which I did over the phone. In 3 <u>days</u>, not weeks, he was completely healed and was able to go to work with no medical intervention. He was glad that he had returned to work the day after the accident because his other supervisor said, "I can't believe that. Are you sure there was something wrong with you? That healed really fast!" But everyone else had already seen him limping in pain and that the injury was real. Eric just answered him, "God!" Thank You Jesus!

Like Baby's Skin

There was a lady at church who asked us to pray for her. The skin on her face was an abnormally dark color, thick and wrinkling. She looked like she was wearing a mask. She said her doctor had diagnosed her with scleroderma, an autoimmune disease that attacks the skin and in some cases the internal organs. It is normally incurable.

We prayed over her that night and declared that she would be healed with evidence that her skin would look like baby's skin. Over the next few months the dark mask started peeling away and her skin became as soft and smooth as a baby's skin. Praise His Name!

Type II Diabetes Cured

A pastor friend of mine called me one day and said, "I went to the doctor today and they have diagnosed me with Type II Diabetes. What should I do?" I believe that the Lord at that point pulled on my medical background and mixed it with His words of wisdom and I told her what to do. In the ensuing days her blood glucose became normal. After 3 months, she went back to the doctor who was surprised and said, "I have never seen this happen. You are no longer a diabetic." Not only that, but the doctor took the diagnosis out of her chart! She said that she had never done that before. When the Lord heals, He heals completely.

Dyslexia Is No Match for Jesus

Richard, a friend of ours, felt the call of God on his life to become a preacher. He wanted to be ordained under Joan Hunter Ministries just as we were. But in order to do that there was quite a number of books that had to be read and studied, as well as many hours of video teaching. The problem was that Richard had dyslexia and reading was extremely difficult for him as anyone with dyslexia can tell you. Reading all those books before the next ordination school would have been impossible for him in the natural. He asked us to pray that he would be able to read the books so he could become ordained.

The Lord answered his request. "It's like being an un-caged animal," he said, "I read so fast my eyes would cross." He could read for hours on end and comprehend what he was reading. When he got done with one book, he just felt compelled to pick up the next one and keep reading. He said he could never do that before. In the next several months he not only read all the books, but had fulfilled all the other perquisites too.

While he was at ordination school, the students all lined up to be prayed for. When Joan laid her hands on him, she prophesied over him. "You have been made fun of because of your short height," she proclaimed, "No more. You are a David that is going to slay many giants." As soon as she said those words the power of God went through him like electricity and he hit the ground shaking. "I have never felt anything like that!" he exclaimed. It has given him confidence like he has never had before.

Right now, as I am writing this, I am watching Richard walking across the stage to receive his Certificate of Ordination. Our God is Lord over every name including dyslexia! When He calls us, He will make a way.

He Is Still Speaking

I was praying this morning on my way to work and thinking about the section in Chapter 8 where we talk about why we don't see everyone we pray for healed. I was asking the Lord to be able to hear Him more clearly for more miracles and healings, not because it makes us look good, but because it shows others His goodness and that He still does miracles and that awakens people to Him.

I started singing, without thinking, "You Make Me Brave" by Amanda Cook. But I was singing, "You call me out beyond the storm into the waves." I thought, "That's not how that goes. It is 'out beyond the shore into the waves.'" Just then the traffic slowed down to a crawl. There was a large truck hauling lumber three vehicles ahead of me. Now we were crawling about 10 miles an hour. I looked down at the license plate on the car directly in front of me and it read, "OFFSHOR1".

I immediately made the connection between the song, the incident with Peter and Jesus walking on the water, and what I had prayed. In my mind I heard the Holy Spirit say, "You are, and need to be more of, an 'OFF SHORE ONE.' One that will ask Me, like Peter, to do the supernatural things I am doing even if others aren't stepping out and doing them. That's where the miraculous happens." And like Peter, I need to do this even if I only get part of it right. Better to take a few steps into the miraculous, than none at all. Jesus is still there to help us and let us know where we went wrong so we do better the next time.

I believe the Lord allowed the traffic to back up so I would pay attention and also so I could take a picture and video of the car. He does things like that. I have included the picture so you can see it for yourself.

I looked up the song when I got to work and found it also says, "So I will let You draw me out beyond the shore into Your grace." The definition of grace I believe the Lord has given to me is this: "The supernatural Presence of God (Holy Spirit) that empowers us to become who we were created to be and to be able to do the works of God." That just gave me chill bumps.

"So then faith cometh by hearing, and hearing by the word of God."
Romans 10:17

Final Words

Heidi and I hope this book has challenged you. God is always speaking. Will you listen? He wants to manifest His Glory on the earth. Will you let Him do that through you? He wants to do things beyond our imagination. Will you do the natural so He can do the supernatural? He is looking for children who will re-present Him well. Will you become one of those sons and daughters that look just like Jesus?

If you answered yes to those questions, then this last verse is for you.

"For the eyes of the LORD run to and fro throughout the whole earth, to show Himself strong on behalf of those whose heart is loyal to Him."

2 Chronicles 16:9

43165337R00084

Made in the USA
Middletown, DE
02 May 2017